Brain-Boosting MATH

Grades 1–2

By Jillayne Prince Wallaker

Cover Design by
Matthew Van Zomeren

Illustrations by
Marty Bucella

Carson-Dellosa Publishing Company, Inc.
Greensboro, North Carolina

Dedication
With love to Maegen, Maddie, Ian, and Willie.

Credits
Author: Jillayne Prince Wallaker
Artist: Marty Bucella
Cover Art Direction: Annette Hollister-Papp
Cover Design: Matthew Van Zomeren
Editors: Kelly Morris Huxmann, Debra Olson Pressnall
Graphic Design and Layout: Mark Conrad

ISBN: 0-88724-932-9

Table of Contents

Table of Contents (continued)

Math Journal (continued)

Name: _____   Date: _____

What is a triangle?
Draw 3 triangles. Draw an arrow pointing to I side and write "3 sides."
Draw an arrow pointing to I angle and write "3 angles."

A _____ is a shape with _____ sides and _____ angles.

The shapes above are _____ because they have

_____ sides and _____ angles.

Name: _____   Date: _____

What is a sum?
Write 2 addition sentences. Draw an arrow to the answers and write "sum."

A _____ is the answer to an addition problem.

In the problems above, _____ and _____ are sums.

Have your students keep math journals following the template presented on pages 6 and 7. Use the premises listed below or generate your own.

To make the journal: Cut a sheet of white paper in half. Staple together to make a four-page booklet. Have students write one premise at the top of each page or cut and paste four of the premises below. Assist students in completing the journal pages. Each journal page must include a premise, an illustration, and an explanation. Evaluate your students' work using the Journal Page Checklist on page 9. Keep one copy for your records and give one copy to the student.

✂ -

What is the value of the number 5?

Prove that 4 is an even number.

Illustrate why $4 - 3 = 1$.

What does the symbol "+" mean?

What is a nickel worth?

What is an AB pattern?

What is $\frac{1}{2}$?

How long is an inch?

Prove that $5 > 2$.

What is the value of the digit 1 in the number 15?

Journal Page Checklist—Teacher Copy

Student name: _____   Date: _____

Evaluated by: _____

- ❏ Student name is at the top.
- ❏ Date is at the top.
- ❏ Premise is written or glued neatly on the page.
- ❏ Illustration fits the premise.
- ❏ Illustration demonstrates understanding of premise.
- ❏ Illustration is neat and easy to understand.
- ❏ Illustration is labeled.
- ❏ Explanation answers the premise.
- ❏ Explanation refers to the illustration.
- ❏ Explanation is neat and easy to read.

Journal Page Checklist—Student Copy

Student name: _____   Date: _____

Evaluated by: _____

- ❏ Student name is at the top.
- ❏ Date is at the top.
- ❏ Premise is written or glued neatly on the page.
- ❏ Illustration fits the premise.
- ❏ Illustration demonstrates understanding of premise.
- ❏ Illustration is neat and easy to understand.
- ❏ Illustration is labeled.
- ❏ Explanation answers the premise.
- ❏ Explanation refers to the illustration.
- ❏ Explanation is neat and easy to read.

Color Correctly

Follow the directions. The first object is always on the left.

1. Color the **first** ladybug red.
    Color the **seventh** ladybug black.
    Color the **ninth** ladybug white.
    Color the **fourth** ladybug yellow.
    Color the **eighth** ladybug brown.

    Color the **fifth** ladybug orange.
    Color the **tenth** ladybug pink.
    Color the **second** ladybug blue.
    Color the **sixth** ladybug purple.
    Color the **third** ladybug green.

2. Color the **sixth** fish green.
    Color the **tenth** fish brown.
    Color the **second** fish pink.
    Color the **eighth** fish orange.
    Color the **first** fish blue.

    Color the **fifth** fish white.
    Color the **third** fish red.
    Color the **ninth** fish purple.
    Color the **seventh** fish yellow.
    Color the **fourth** fish black.

CD-4333 *Brain-Boosting Math*

Color Correctly (continued)

Make your own. Share with a friend.
Fill in the first blank with an ordinal number:

| first | second | third | fourth | fifth | sixth | seventh | eighth | ninth | tenth |

Do not write them in order. Fill in the second blank with a color word.

Color the _____ circle _____ .

Color the _____ circle _____ .

Color the _____ circle _____ .

Color the _____ circle _____ .

Color the _____ circle _____ .

Color the _____ circle _____ .

Color the _____ circle _____ .

Color the _____ circle _____ .

Color the _____ circle _____ .

Color the _____ circle _____ .

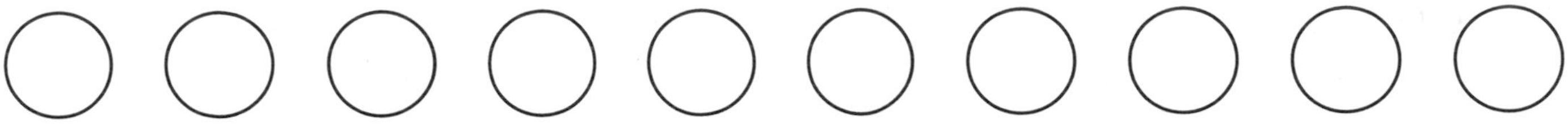

◯ ◯ ◯ ◯ ◯ ◯ ◯ ◯ ◯ ◯

CD-4333 *Brain-Boosting Math*

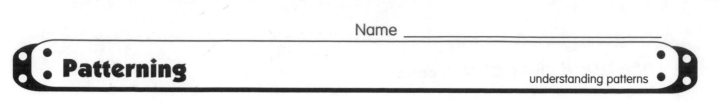

Patterning

Patterns are made up of 2 things: pieces and a sequence.

● The pieces are the parts of the pattern. In the patterns below, the circle and the square are each a piece. Call the circle **A** and the square **B**.

● The sequence of a pattern is the order of its pieces. The pattern on the left is an **AB** pattern. The pattern on the right is an **ABB** pattern.

Name each pattern. Then, make the same pattern using different shapes. Draw your new pattern below the original one.

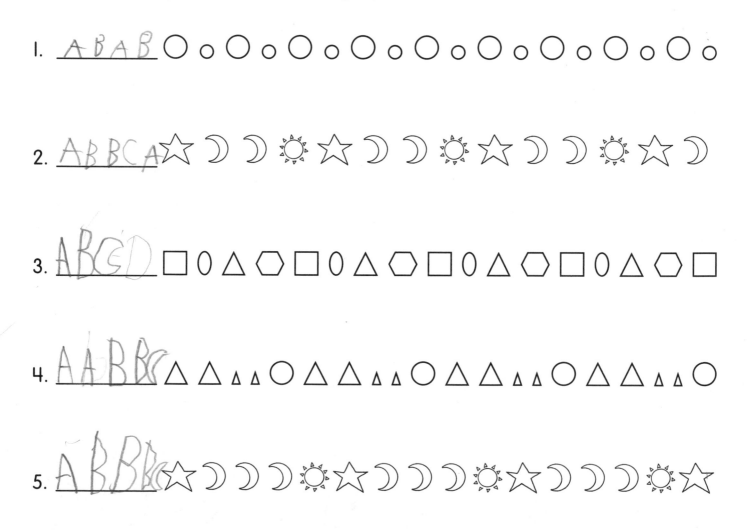

1. _A B A B_

2. _A B B C A_

3. _A B C D_

4. _A A B B_

5. _A B B B_

Leapfrog

Write the numbers from smallest to largest on the frogs. Start on the left.
Write other numbers between the frogs. Keep the numbers in order.

A. 25, 6, 18, 44

B. 52, 100, 96, 65

C. 405, 179, 281, 103

D. 768, 537, 601, 670

E. 347, 220, 383, 374

CD-4333 *Brain-Boosting Math*

Quackers

Make as many numbers as you can using all the digits in the eggs. Write the largest number in the first duckling. Write the smallest number in the last duckling. Write 2 other numbers in the middle ducklings in order from largest to smallest.

A. (eggs: 2, 8, 7)

B. (eggs: 1, 3, 9)

C. (eggs: 4, 9, 6)

D. (eggs: 2, 5, 1, 7)

E. (eggs: 3, 8, 4, 6)

F. Write your own digits in the eggs. Fill in the ducklings.

CD-4333 *Brain-Boosting Math*

Higher or Lower?

Play Higher or Lower. Use the clues to find the mystery number.

GAME 1

I have a number between 1 and 100.
Guess: (50) 0   105
Clue: higher
It is between _50_ and _100_ .

Read to find the range.

Circle the best guess.

Read the clue. The number is higher than the best guess (50).

Fill in the new range. Continue playing the game.

A. Guess: 46   75   101
Clue: lower
It is between _____ and _____ .

B. Guess: 32   65   83
Clue: lower
It is between _____ and _____ .

C. Guess: 56   69   73
Clue: higher
It is between _____ and _____ .

D. Guess: 49   55   60
Clue: higher
It is between _____ and _____ .

E. Guess: 63   66   69
Clue: lower
It is between _____ and _____ .

F. Guess: 57   61   64
Clue: higher
It is between _____ and _____ .

The number is _____ .

GAME 2

I have a number between 20 and 80.

A. Guess: 16   60   81
Clue: lower
It is between _____ and _____ .

B. Guess: 35   63   72
Clue: lower
It is between _____ and _____ .

C. Guess: 19   26   36
Clue: higher
It is between _____ and _____ .

D. Guess: 23   29   35
Clue: lower
It is between _____ and _____ .

E. Guess: 26   28   33
Clue: lower
It is between _____ and _____ .

The number is _____ .

Numbers in the Box

place value/number sense

Use the numbers below to answer the questions.

| 578 | 341 | 259 | 97 | 820 | 443 |

1. Write the number.

   a. Which number has a 2 in the tens place? _____

   b. Which number has a 4 in the hundreds place? _____

   c. Which number has an 8 in the ones place? _____

   d. Which number has a 5 in the hundreds place? _____

2. In your head—which number works?

   a. Add 100 and get 441. _____

   b. Add 2 and get 580. _____

   c. Subtract 400 and get 43. _____

   d. Subtract 10 and get 810. _____

3. Even or odd?

   a. List the even numbers. _____

   b. List the odd numbers. _____

4. Put them in order.

   a. Order the numbers from smallest to largest.

   _____, _____, _____, _____, _____, _____

   b. Order the numbers from largest to smallest.

   _____, _____, _____, _____, _____, _____

CD-4333 *Brain-Boosting Math*

Numbers in the Box (continued)

Use the numbers below to answer the questions.

| 578 | 341 | 259 | 97 | 820 | 443 |

5. Each number above is written in **standard form**. Write the standard form of each number on the line in the box. Then, sketch the picture form of each number. The first one has been done for you.

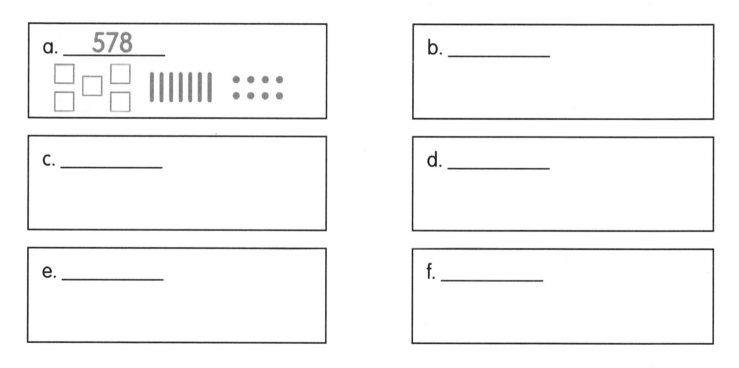

a. __578__

b. _____

c. _____

d. _____

e. _____

f. _____

6. Use each number at least once to make true comparisons.

a. _____ > _____

b. _____ > _____

c. _____ > _____

d. _____ < _____

e. _____ = _____

f. _____ = _____

Done

Put It Away

Use the coordinates to help Tidy Tim put away his things.
Cut out the pictures along the dotted lines and paste them on the dresser.

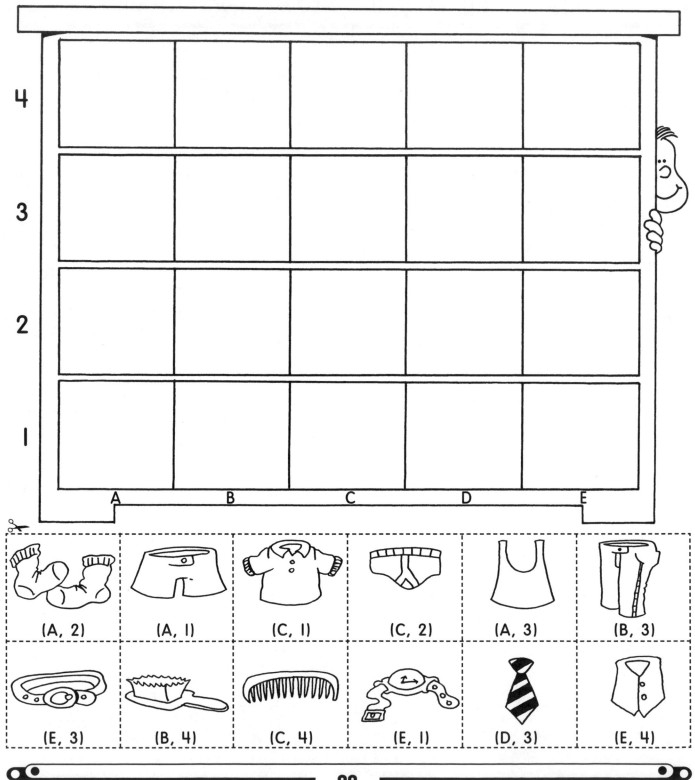

(A, 2)	(A, 1)	(C, 1)	(C, 2)	(A, 3)	(B, 3)
(E, 3)	(B, 4)	(C, 4)	(E, 1)	(D, 3)	(E, 4)

Bagglers' Bins

Help Bimmie and Buggie Baggler find their things. Write the coordinates of the bin that contains each object. Remember to go across first, then up.

A. 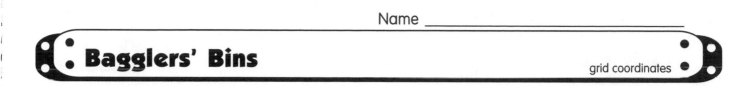 (,)   B. (,)

C. (,)   D. (,)

E. (,)   F. (,)

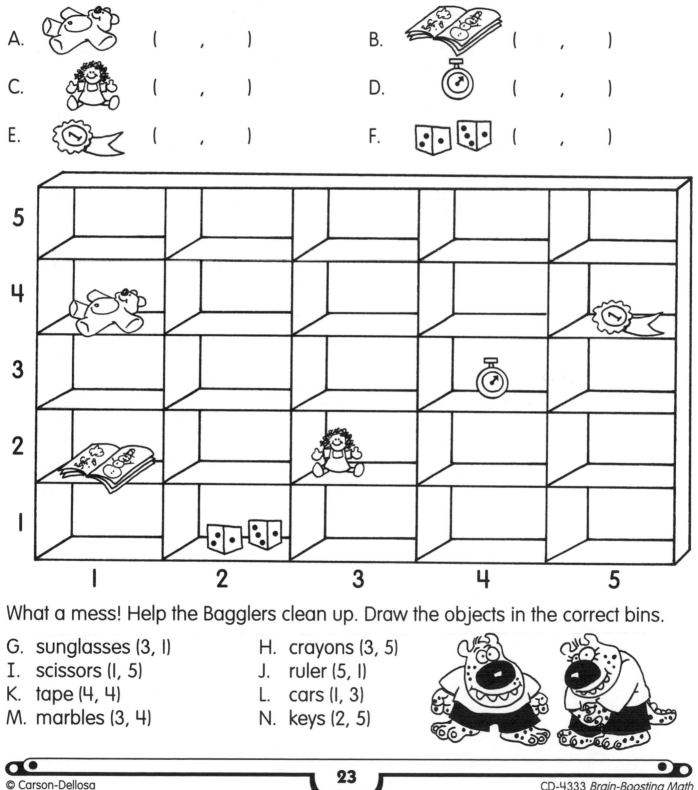

What a mess! Help the Bagglers clean up. Draw the objects in the correct bins.

G. sunglasses (3, 1)   H. crayons (3, 5)
I. scissors (1, 5)   J. ruler (5, 1)
K. tape (4, 4)   L. cars (1, 3)
M. marbles (3, 4)   N. keys (2, 5)

CD-4333 *Brain-Boosting Math*

Is It Certain?

How likely is each event? Circle **certain**, **impossible**, or **maybe**.

Color I red. Color 4 yellow.

I.	First pick white	certain	impossible	maybe
2.	First pick yellow	certain	impossible	maybe
3.	One red out, next pick red	certain	impossible	maybe
4.	One red out, next pick yellow	certain	impossible	maybe
5.	One yellow out, next pick red	certain	impossible	maybe

Color 3 blue. Color 2 purple.

6.	First pick purple	certain	impossible	maybe
7.	First pick red	certain	impossible	maybe
8.	Two purple out, next pick purple	certain	impossible	maybe
9.	Two blue out, next pick blue	certain	impossible	maybe
10.	Three blue out, next pick purple	certain	impossible	maybe

CD-4333 *Brain-Boosting Math*

Is It Certain? (continued)

11. First pick zebra	certain	impossible	maybe
12. Zebra up, next pick elephant	certain	impossible	maybe
13. Zebra up, next pick zebra	certain	impossible	maybe
14. Zebra and elephant up, next pick monkey	certain	impossible	maybe
15. Zebra, elephant, and lion up, next pick ostrich	certain	impossible	maybe

16. First pick potato	certain	impossible	maybe
17. First pick lettuce	certain	impossible	maybe
18. Lettuce up, next pick carrot	certain	impossible	maybe
19. Lettuce and carrot up, next pick bean	certain	impossible	maybe
20. Lettuce and bean up, next pick carrot	certain	impossible	maybe

CD-4333 *Brain-Boosting Math*

Predict

What will happen if I object is picked from the bag? Follow the directions.
Then, draw 2 lines to match the most likely and least likely results.

1. Color 2 red.
   Color 9 blue.

   red

   blue

   most likely pick

   least likely pick

2. Color 2 yellow.
   Color 5 orange.
   Color 3 black.

   yellow

   orange

   black

   most likely pick

   least likely pick

3. Color I white.
   Color 4 green.
   Color 7 yellow.

   white

   green

   yellow

   most likely pick

   least likely pick

4. Color 8 purple.
   Color I pink.
   Color 3 blue.

   purple

   pink

   blue

   most likely pick

   least likely pick

5. Use 2 colors
   to color the
   squares.

   _____

   _____

   most likely pick

   least likely pick

6. Use 3 colors
   to color the
   squares.

   _____

   _____

   _____

   most likely pick

   least likely pick

Tic-Tac-Time

Write the time below each clock. Then, look at the list of digital times. Draw an **X** on the clocks that match the digital times. Draw an **O** on the clocks that do not match. Write **X** or **O** on the line to show who won each game.

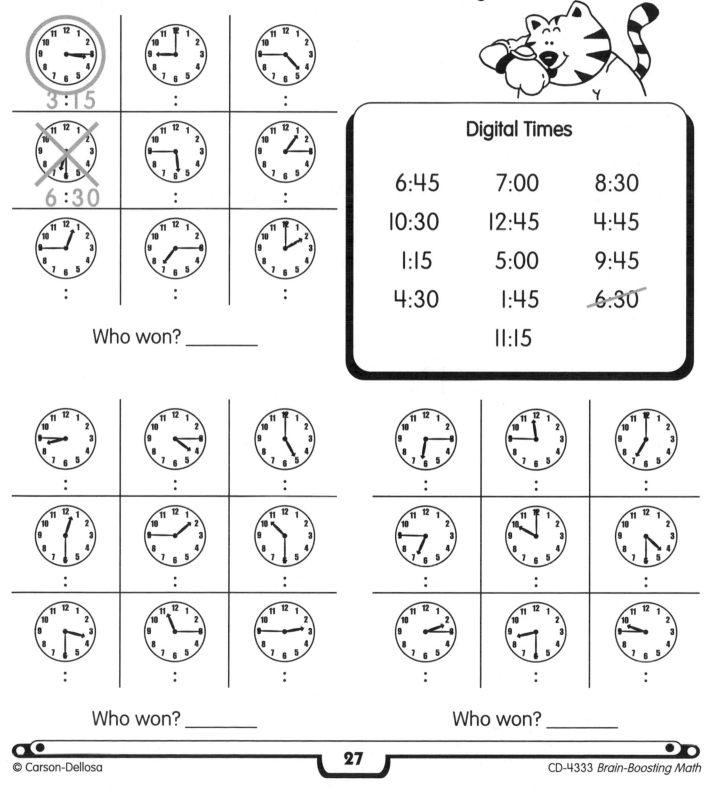

Digital Times

6:45	7:00	8:30
10:30	12:45	4:45
1:15	5:00	9:45
4:30	1:45	~~6:30~~
	11:15	

Who won? _____

Who won? _____   Who won? _____

Clock Shop

Write the time under each clock. Follow the directions.

1. Find the time
   in I hour.

   Circle it with red. ___ : ___

2. Find the time
   in I hour.

   Circle it with blue. ___ : ___

3. Find the time
   I hour ago.

   Box it with orange. ___ : ___

4. Find the time
   I hour ago.

   Box it with yellow. ___ : ___

5. Find the time
   in I hour.

   Circle it with yellow. ___ : ___

6. Find the time
   in I hour.

   Circle it with green. ___ : ___

7. Find the time
   I hour ago.

   Box it with purple. ___ : ___

8. Find the time
   I hour ago.

   Box it with blue. ___ : ___

9. Find the time
   in I hour.

   Circle it with orange. ___ : ___

10. Find the time
    in I hour.

    Circle it with purple. ___ : ___

11. Find the time
    I hour ago.

    Box it with red. ___ : ___

12. Find the time
    I hour ago.

    Box it with green. ___ : ___

High Five

Look at the clock. Starting at the top, count by 5s. Write the multiples of 5 in the boxes to show the minutes. Then, answer the questions.

How many minutes . . .

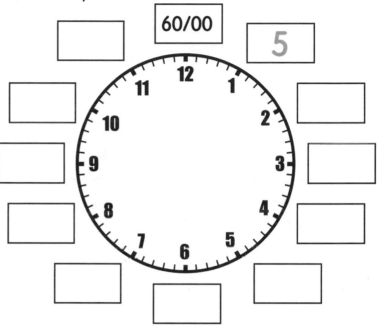

60/00

5

1. between 1:00 and 1:10?

   _____

2. between 3:00 and 3:05?

   _____

3. between 12:00 and 12:45?

   _____

4. between 4:00 and 4:30?

   _____

5. Put your finger on the 3.
   Count by 5s until you get to the 7.
   What is your count?

   _____

   This is the amount of time that passed between 2:15 and 2:35.

6. How many minutes between 5:30 and 5:45?   _____

7. How many minutes between 7:20 and 7:30?   _____

8. How many minutes between 1:10 and 1:30?   _____

9. How many minutes between 8:35 and 8:40?   _____

10. How many minutes between 6:15 and 6:35?   _____

11. How many minutes between 10:55 and 11:00?   _____

12. How many minutes between 11:45 and 12:05?   _____

CD-4333 *Brain-Boosting Math*

School Schedule

Circle the best answer. How long does it take . . .

1.	to eat lunch?	15 minutes	15 hours
2.	to sharpen a pencil?	20 seconds	20 minutes
3.	to say the alphabet?	1 second	1 minute
4.	to watch a movie?	2 minutes	2 hours

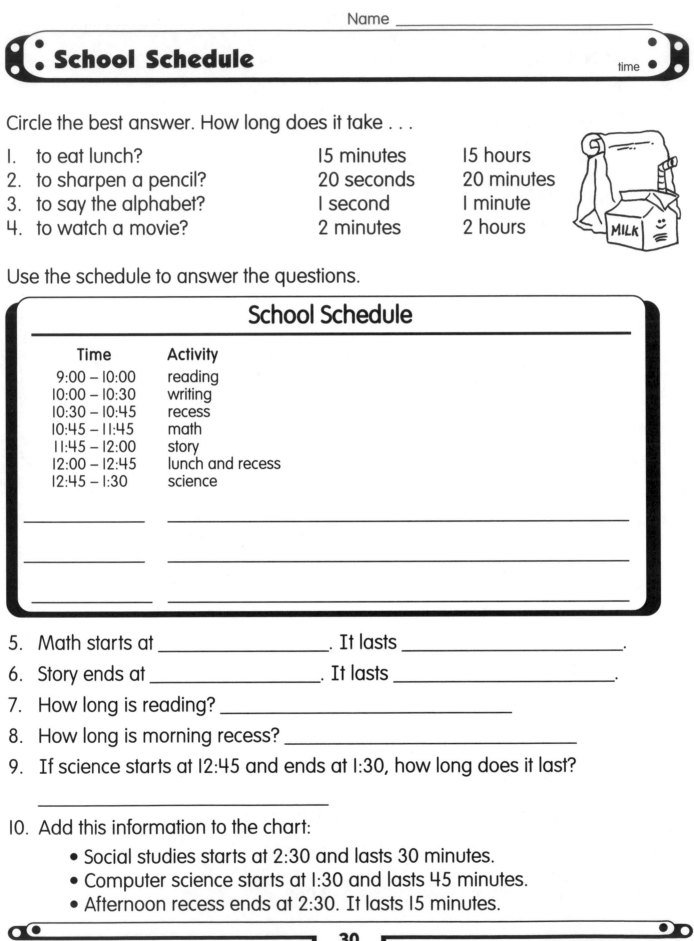

Use the schedule to answer the questions.

School Schedule

Time	Activity
9:00 – 10:00	reading
10:00 – 10:30	writing
10:30 – 10:45	recess
10:45 – 11:45	math
11:45 – 12:00	story
12:00 – 12:45	lunch and recess
12:45 – 1:30	science

_____   _____

_____   _____

_____   _____

5. Math starts at _____. It lasts _____.

6. Story ends at _____. It lasts _____.

7. How long is reading? _____

8. How long is morning recess? _____

9. If science starts at 12:45 and ends at 1:30, how long does it last?

_____

10. Add this information to the chart:

  • Social studies starts at 2:30 and lasts 30 minutes.
  • Computer science starts at 1:30 and lasts 45 minutes.
  • Afternoon recess ends at 2:30. It lasts 15 minutes.

CD-4333 *Brain-Boosting Math*

Calendar Page

using a calendar

Look at the calendar. Fill in the missing numbers. Then, answer the questions.

March

Sunday	Monday	Tuesday	Wednesday	Thursday	Friday	Saturday
				1	2	3
25						31

1. What month does this calendar show? _____

2. On what day of the week does this month begin? _____

3. On what day of the week does this month end? _____

4. Put an X on the first Wednesday. What is the date? _____

5. Ria's birthday is on the second Tuesday. Mark her birthday on the calendar with a B. What is the date? _____

6. Color the 12th blue. What day of the week is it? _____

   What is the date one week before? _____

7. Color the Fridays yellow. How many are there? _____

8. Spring vacation begins on the last Friday. Mark the day on the calendar with a star. What is the date? _____

CD-4333 *Brain-Boosting Math*

In a Year

Look at the calendar. Answer the questions.

January
S	M	T	W	T	F	S
			1	2	3	4
5	6	7	8	9	10	11
12	13	14	15	16	17	18
19	20	21	22	23	24	25
26	27	28	29	30	31	

February
S	M	T	W	T	F	S
						1
2	3	4	5	6	7	8
9	10	11	12	13	14	15
16	17	18	19	20	21	22
23	24	25	26	27	28	

March
S	M	T	W	T	F	S
						1
2	3	4	5	6	7	8
9	10	11	12	13	14	15
16	17	18	19	20	21	22
23/30	24/31	25	26	27	28	29

April
S	M	T	W	T	F	S
		1	2	3	4	5
6	7	8	9	10	11	12
13	14	15	16	17	18	19
20	21	22	23	24	25	26
27	28	29	30			

May
S	M	T	W	T	F	S
				1	2	3
4	5	6	7	8	9	10
11	12	13	14	15	16	17
18	19	20	21	22	23	24
25	26	27	28	29	30	31

June
S	M	T	W	T	F	S
1	2	3	4	5	6	7
8	9	10	11	12	13	14
15	16	17	18	19	20	21
22	23	24	25	26	27	28
29	30					

July
S	M	T	W	T	F	S
		1	2	3	4	5
6	7	8	9	10	11	12
13	14	15	16	17	18	19
20	21	22	23	24	25	26
27	28	29	30	31		

August
S	M	T	W	T	F	S
					1	2
3	4	5	6	7	8	9
10	11	12	13	14	15	16
17	18	19	20	21	22	23
24/31	25	26	27	28	29	30

September
S	M	T	W	T	F	S
	1	2	3	4	5	6
7	8	9	10	11	12	13
14	15	16	17	18	19	20
21	22	23	24	25	26	27
28	29	30				

October
S	M	T	W	T	F	S
			1	2	3	4
5	6	7	8	9	10	11
12	13	14	15	16	17	18
19	20	21	22	23	24	25
26	27	28	29	30	31	

November
S	M	T	W	T	F	S
						1
2	3	4	5	6	7	8
9	10	11	12	13	14	15
16	17	18	19	20	21	22
23/30	24	25	26	27	28	29

December
S	M	T	W	T	F	S
	1	2	3	4	5	6
7	8	9	10	11	12	13
14	15	16	17	18	19	20
21	22	23	24	25	26	27
28	29	30	31			

1. Color the months with 31 days blue. Color the months with 30 days green.

2. What month does not have 31 or 30 days? _____

3. What month comes right after February? _____

4. What month comes right after October? _____

5. What month comes right before May? _____

6. What month comes right before September? _____

7. School ends the sixth month. What is the sixth month? _____

8. What month comes 2 months after January? _____

9. What is the fifth month of the year? _____

10. How many months are there in 1 year? _____

Show the Sum

addition with two or three addends

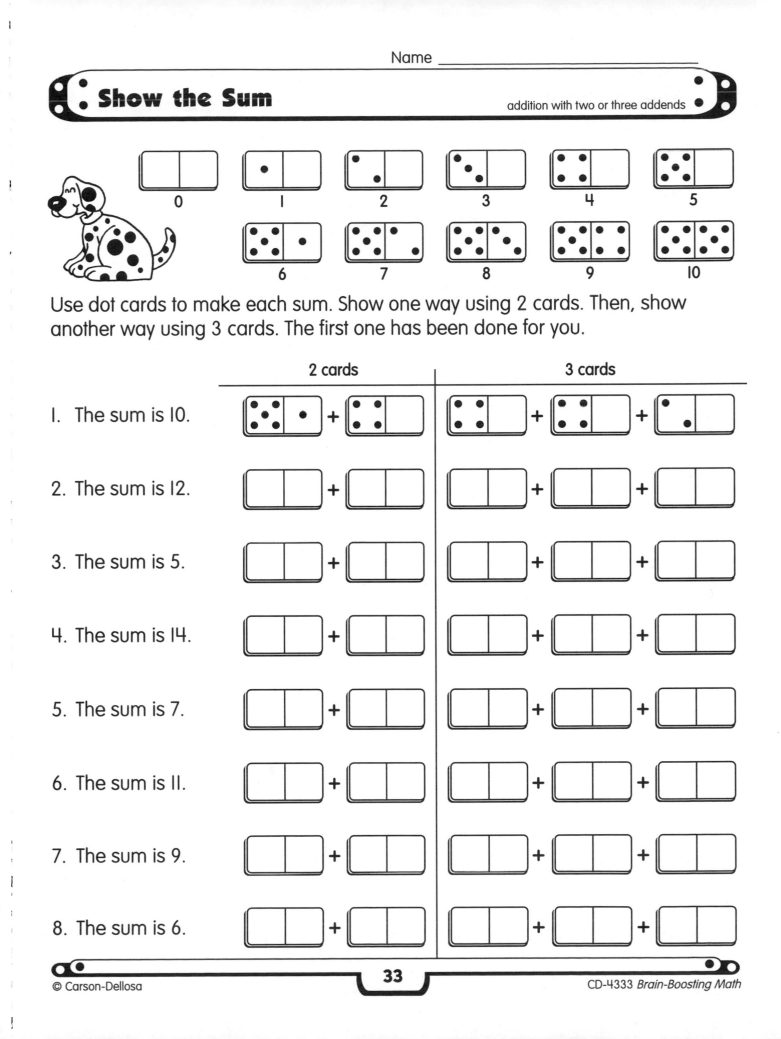

Use dot cards to make each sum. Show one way using 2 cards. Then, show another way using 3 cards. The first one has been done for you.

	2 cards	3 cards
1. The sum is 10.		
2. The sum is 12.		
3. The sum is 5.		
4. The sum is 14.		
5. The sum is 7.		
6. The sum is 11.		
7. The sum is 9.		
8. The sum is 6.		

Going Buggy

Solve. Then, follow the directions to color the bugs.

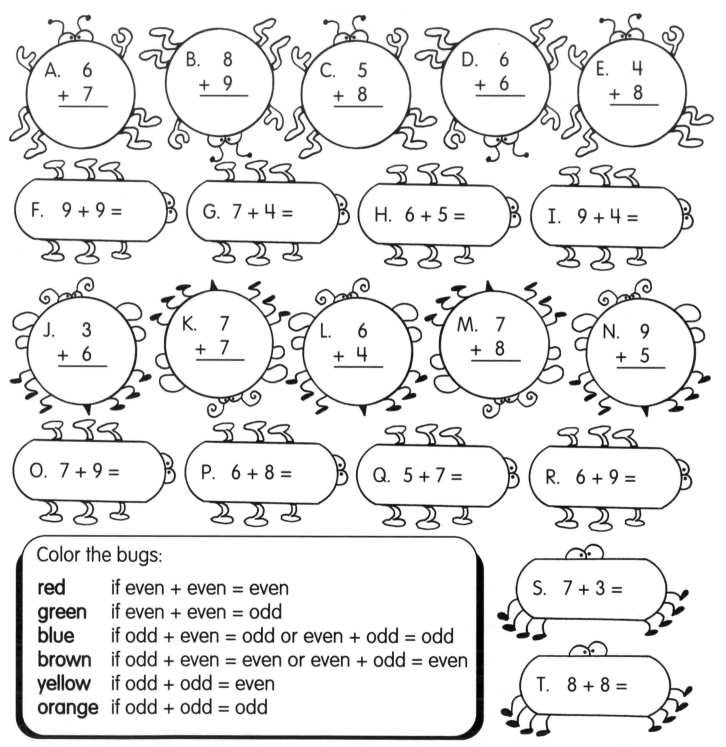

A. 6 + 7

B. 8 + 9

C. 5 + 8

D. 6 + 6

E. 4 + 8

F. 9 + 9 =

G. 7 + 4 =

H. 6 + 5 =

I. 9 + 4 =

J. 3 + 6

K. 7 + 7

L. 6 + 4

M. 7 + 8

N. 9 + 5

O. 7 + 9 =

P. 6 + 8 =

Q. 5 + 7 =

R. 6 + 9 =

Color the bugs:

red   if even + even = even
green   if even + even = odd
blue   if odd + even = odd or even + odd = odd
brown   if odd + even = even or even + odd = even
yellow   if odd + odd = even
orange   if odd + odd = odd

S. 7 + 3 =

T. 8 + 8 =

What did you notice when you colored the bugs? Share your ideas.

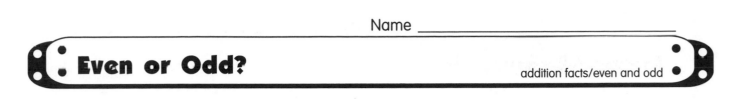

Even or Odd?

addition facts/even and odd

Solve. Write **E** in the box if the number is even. Write **O** if the number is odd.

A. 3 □
    + 5 □
       □

B. 0 □
    + 3 □
       □

C. 4 □
    + 5 □
       □

D. 5 □
    + 8 □
       □

E. 6 + 5 =
    □ □ □

F. 3 + 1 =
    □ □ □

G. 2 + 6 =
    □ □ □

H. 8 + 7 =
    □ □ □

I. 9 + 2 =
    □ □ □

J. 4 □
    + 6 □
       □

K. 5 □
    + 5 □
       □

L. 9 □
    + 4 □
       □

M. 2 □
    + 2 □
       □

N. 7 + 9 =
    □ □ □

O. 3 + 7 =
    □ □ □

P. 6 + 6 =
    □ □ □

Q. 7 + 5 =
    □ □ □

R. 1 + 4 =
    □ □ □

Circle every problem with an even sum. Then, look at the problems you circled and check each true statement below.

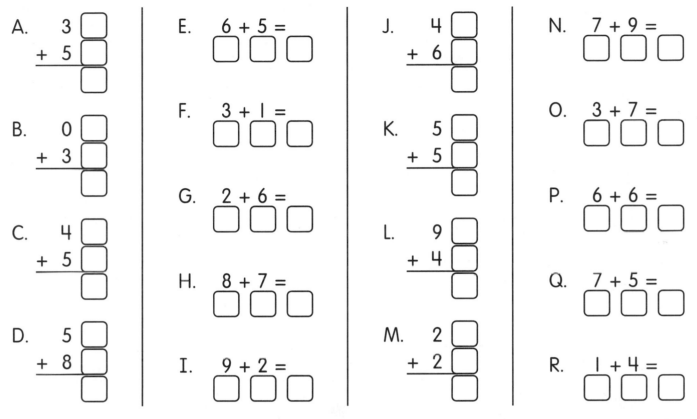

___ Two even addends have an even sum.

___ There is no pattern to the problems with even sums.

___ An even and an odd addend have an even sum.

___ Two odd addends have an even sum.

What do you notice about the addends of problems with odd sums?

_____

Try other addition problems. Predict whether the sums will be even or odd.

CD-4333 *Brain-Boosting Math*

Picture Subtraction

Look at the pictures. Complete the tables.
Write each number sentence and find the answer.

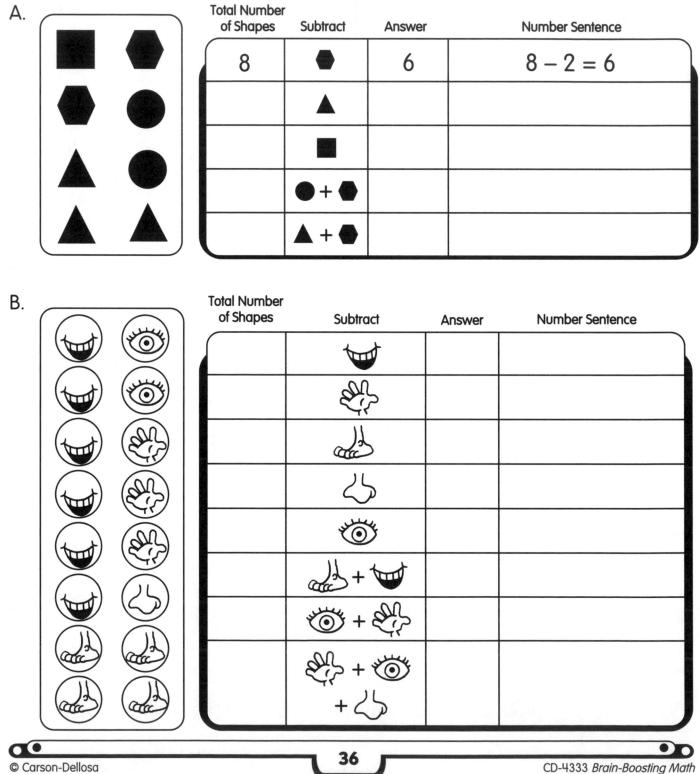

A.

Total Number of Shapes	Subtract	Answer	Number Sentence
8	⬡	6	8 – 2 = 6
	▲		
	■		
	● + ⬡		
	▲ + ⬡		

B.

Total Number of Shapes	Subtract	Answer	Number Sentence
	😀		
	✋		
	👣		
	👃		
	👁		
	👣 + 😀		
	👁 + ✋		
	✋ + 👁 + 👃		

CD-4333 *Brain-Boosting Math*

Who's Greater?

Subtract. Write the answer above each problem. Circle <, >, or =.

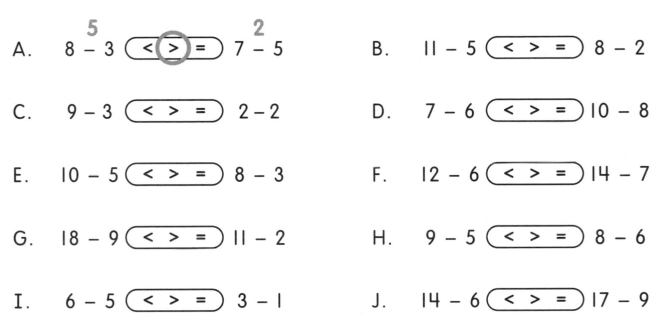

A. 8 – 3 (< **>** =) 7 – 5   B. 11 – 5 (< > =) 8 – 2

C. 9 – 3 (< > =) 2 – 2   D. 7 – 6 (< > =) 10 – 8

E. 10 – 5 (< > =) 8 – 3   F. 12 – 6 (< > =) 14 – 7

G. 18 – 9 (< > =) 11 – 2   H. 9 – 5 (< > =) 8 – 6

I. 6 – 5 (< > =) 3 – 1   J. 14 – 6 (< > =) 17 – 9

Make a graph. Color one square for each symbol used above.

Symbol	Number of Times Used									
<	□	□	□	□	□	□	□	□	□	□
>	□	□	□	□	□	□	□	□	□	□
=	□	□	□	□	□	□	□	□	□	□

Circle **True** or **False**.

K.   **True**   **False**   = was used the most

L.   **True**   **False**   < was used more often than =

M.   **True**   **False**   > was used less often than <

N.   **True**   **False**   < was used as often as =

    CD-4333 *Brain-Boosting Math*

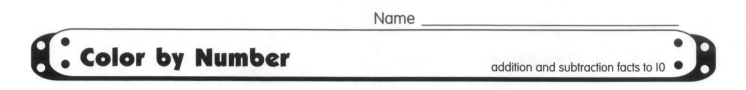

Color by Number

addition and subtraction facts to 10

Solve the problems. Use your answers to color the picture:

2 = blue   4 = brown   5 = yellow   6 = purple
7 = green   8 = orange   9 = pink   10 = red

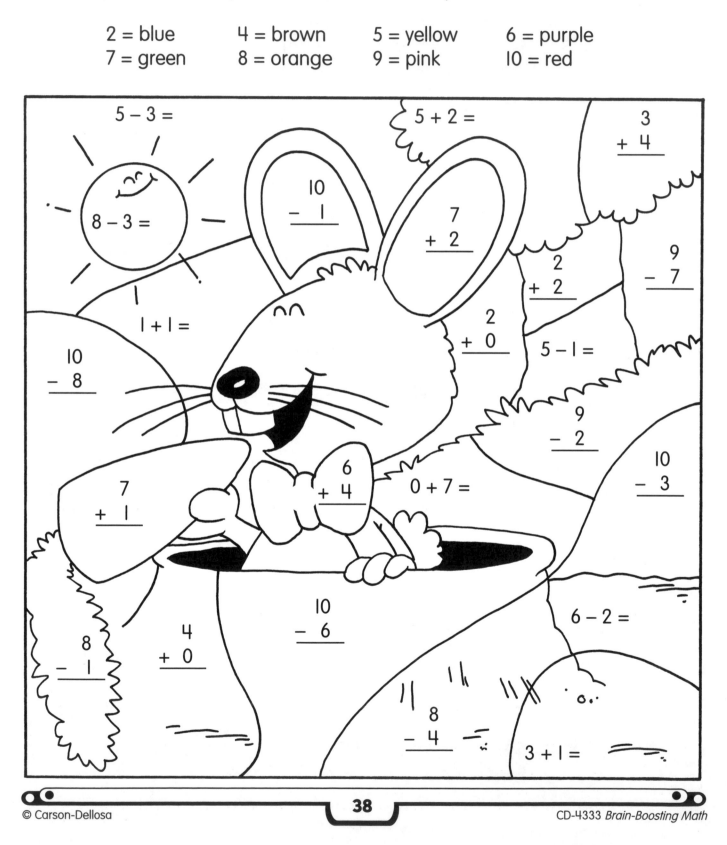

$5 - 3 =$

$5 + 2 =$

$3 + 4$

$8 - 3 =$

$10 - 1$

$7 + 2$

$9 - 7$

$1 + 1 =$

$2 + 2$

$10 - 8$

$2 + 0$

$5 - 1 =$

$9 - 2$

$7 + 1$

$6 + 4$

$0 + 7 =$

$10 - 3$

$8 - 1$

$4 + 0$

$10 - 6$

$6 - 2 =$

$8 - 4$

$3 + 1 =$

CD-4333 *Brain-Boosting Math*

Color by Number (continued)

Create your own color-by-number picture.

1. Draw a picture or cut and paste a coloring book page in the frame below.

2. Choose 5–12 colors to use in the picture. Assign a number to each color. Write each number in a crayon. Color the crayon the correct color.

3. Decide what color each part of the picture should be. Write a problem whose answer is that number. For example, if 3 is black and you want a black tire, write **6 – 3 =** inside the tire. Write a problem for each space.

4. Outline everything with a thin black marker or pen.

5. Trade with a partner.

Spiders

Ernie and Jade are playing a game called Spider. The first player with 8 legs on the spider wins. Solve the problems. Circle each problem with an answer of 8. Draw I leg on the spider for each circled answer.

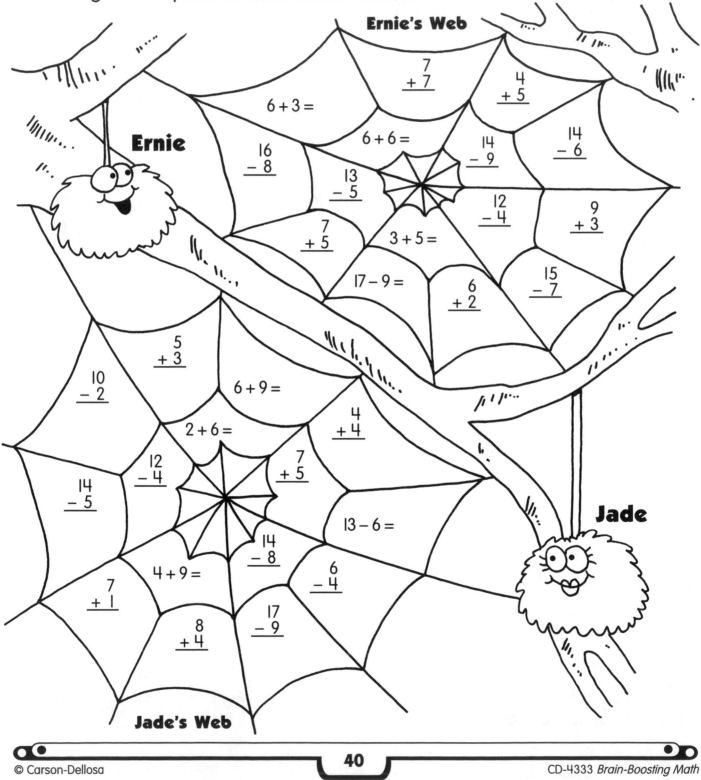

Ernie's Web

Ernie

$6 + 3 =$

$7 + 7$

$4 + 5$

$6 + 6 =$

$\begin{array}{r} 16 \\ -\ 8 \end{array}$

$\begin{array}{r} 14 \\ -\ 9 \end{array}$

$\begin{array}{r} 14 \\ -\ 6 \end{array}$

$\begin{array}{r} 13 \\ -\ 5 \end{array}$

$\begin{array}{r} 12 \\ -\ 4 \end{array}$

$\begin{array}{r} 9 \\ +\ 3 \end{array}$

$7 + 5$

$3 + 5 =$

$17 - 9 =$

$\begin{array}{r} 6 \\ +\ 2 \end{array}$

$\begin{array}{r} 15 \\ -\ 7 \end{array}$

$\begin{array}{r} 5 \\ +\ 3 \end{array}$

$\begin{array}{r} 10 \\ -\ 2 \end{array}$

$6 + 9 =$

$\begin{array}{r} 4 \\ +\ 4 \end{array}$

$2 + 6 =$

$\begin{array}{r} 12 \\ -\ 4 \end{array}$

$\begin{array}{r} 7 \\ +\ 5 \end{array}$

$\begin{array}{r} 14 \\ -\ 5 \end{array}$

$13 - 6 =$

Jade

$\begin{array}{r} 14 \\ -\ 8 \end{array}$

$4 + 9 =$

$\begin{array}{r} 6 \\ -\ 4 \end{array}$

$\begin{array}{r} 7 \\ +\ 1 \end{array}$

$\begin{array}{r} 8 \\ +\ 4 \end{array}$

$\begin{array}{r} 17 \\ -\ 9 \end{array}$

Jade's Web

CD-4333 *Brain-Boosting Math*

:Bead It

Color the beads. Use the beads to write the addition and subtraction fact families.

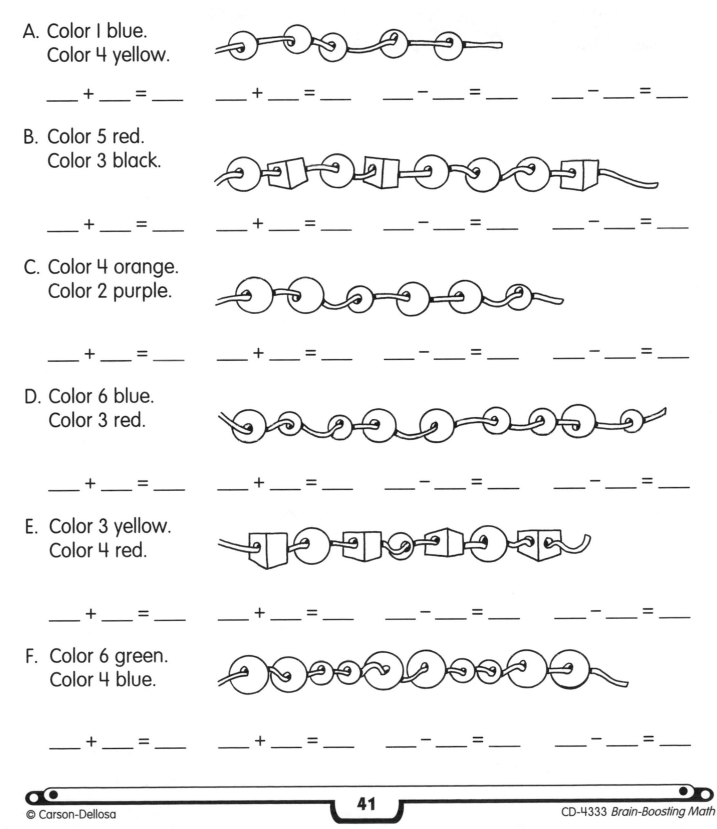

A. Color 1 blue.
   Color 4 yellow.

___ + ___ = ___   ___ + ___ = ___   ___ − ___ = ___   ___ − ___ = ___

B. Color 5 red.
   Color 3 black.

___ + ___ = ___   ___ + ___ = ___   ___ − ___ = ___   ___ − ___ = ___

C. Color 4 orange.
   Color 2 purple.

___ + ___ = ___   ___ + ___ = ___   ___ − ___ = ___   ___ − ___ = ___

D. Color 6 blue.
   Color 3 red.

___ + ___ = ___   ___ + ___ = ___   ___ − ___ = ___   ___ − ___ = ___

E. Color 3 yellow.
   Color 4 red.

___ + ___ = ___   ___ + ___ = ___   ___ − ___ = ___   ___ − ___ = ___

F. Color 6 green.
   Color 4 blue.

___ + ___ = ___   ___ + ___ = ___   ___ − ___ = ___   ___ − ___ = ___

Addition Table

addition and subtraction

Name _____

Fill in the table. Look at the problems on the right. Follow the directions below.

+	0	1	2	3	4	5	6	7	8	9	10
0	0										
1			3								
2											
3							9				
4											
5											
6											
7		8									
8											
9											
10											

Problems:

11 − 9	5 + 6
5 + 5	5 − 1
15 − 10	2 + 3
7 + 3	15 − 6
15 − 9	11 − 4
2 + 5	2 + 7
17 − 7	11 − 2
9 − 7	3 + 4
12 − 4	5 + 3
8 − 4	1 + 1
6 − 5	2 + 9
2 + 2	8 − 3

A. Circle ways to make 10 with yellow. _____

B. Circle ways to make 7 with blue. _____

C. Circle ways to make 4 with orange. _____

D. Circle ways to make 9 with red. _____

E. Circle ways to make 2 with purple. _____

F. Circle ways to make 5 with green. _____

G. On the lines above, write another number sentence to make each number. Use + and −.

CD-4333 *Brain-Boosting Math*

Pathway

Solve. Compare each set of answers. Write <, >, or = in the circle.
Color the squares to find the red pathway: green if <, blue if =, red if >.

5
+ 6   7
     + 8
◯
	16
	− 8 5
	     + 2
	◯
		4
		+ 8 10
		     − 5
		◯
			7
			+ 3 9
			     + 2
			◯

7
+ 4   6
     + 6
◯
	8
	+ 4 5
	     + 7
	◯
		18
		− 9 4
		     + 4
		◯
			5
			+ 4 17
			     − 8
			◯

6
+ 7   9
     + 8
◯
	4
	+ 7 6
	     + 5
	◯
		4
		+ 9 11
		     − 2
		◯
			3
			+ 4 12
			     − 4
			◯

8
+ 2   4
     + 7
◯
	3
	+ 9 15
	     − 8
	◯
		9
		+ 5 15
		     − 6
		◯
			15
			− 7 3
			     + 5
			◯

3
+ 4   14
     − 7
◯
	5
	+ 6 14
	     − 6
	◯
		3
		+ 3 16
		     − 9
		◯
			11
			− 4 3
			     + 9
			◯

CD-4333 *Brain-Boosting Math*

Tic-Tac-Toe

Solve. Put an **O** on problems with an odd answer.
Put an **X** on problems with an even answer. Who won each game?

6 + 4	7 + 2	2 + 4
6 + 8	5 + 6	3 + 8
7 + 3	4 + 8	9 + 4

15 − 8	14 − 6	9 − 5
16 − 8	11 − 4	8 − 2
10 − 7	13 − 8	12 − 3

3 + 8	8 − 2	9 + 4
6 + 6	2 + 9	15 − 9
12 − 4	16 − 7	4 + 9

1 + 8	10 − 6	11 − 5
9 + 4	4 + 3	13 − 7
4 + 6	15 − 6	3 + 7

5 + 6	12 − 7	4 + 8
7 + 8	8 − 6	8 + 0
9 − 2	14 − 6	2 + 7

13 − 4	14 − 6	9 + 5
5 + 5	7 + 8	13 − 8
2 + 9	8 + 3	7 + 5

8 + 4	14 − 8	3 + 8
18 − 9	11 − 9	4 + 4
3 + 6	2 + 2	13 − 6

12 − 4	13 − 8	6 + 9
3 + 9	7 + 4	11 − 2
9 + 5	15 − 7	5 + 7

Make a tally chart to show who won the most games.

even	
odd	
no one	

Chain of Equalities

Look at each chain of equalities. Circle the part that does not belong.
Add one equal number sentence to the end of the chain.

A. $9 + 7 = 16 = 8 + 8 = 14 + 3 = 10 + 6 =$ ☐ ○ ☐

B. $10 = 5 + 5 = 3 + 8 = 9 + 1 = 14 - 4 =$ ☐ ○ ☐

C. $4 + 6 = 5 = 8 - 3 = 1 + 4 = 3 + 2 =$ ☐ ○ ☐

D. $6 + 6 = 7 + 5 = 2 + 9 = 12 = 4 + 8 =$ ☐ ○ ☐

E. $17 - 8 = 15 - 6 = 3 + 6 = 8 = 4 + 5 =$ ☐ ○ ☐

F. $6 - 3 = 9 - 6 = 2 + 1 = 7 + 1 = 10 - 7 =$ ☐ ○ ☐

G. $6 = 5 + 2 = 8 - 2 = 12 - 6 = 3 + 3 =$ ☐ ○ ☐

H. $3 + 4 = 7 = 11 - 3 = 6 + 1 = 12 - 5 =$ ☐ ○ ☐

Make your own chain of equalities. Add as many links as you can.
How many links can you make?

_____

_____

_____

_____

Operation

Write **+** or **−** on the line to make each number sentence true.

A. 3 ____ 3 = 6   B. 7 ____ 2 = 5   C. 4 ____ 8 = 12

D. 6 ____ 4 = 10   E. 6 ____ 4 = 2   F. 15 ____ 9 = 6

G. 5 ____ 7 = 12   H. 10 ____ 7 = 3   I. 6 ____ 9 = 15

J. 7 ____ 6 = 13   K. 16 ____ 8 = 8   L. 4 ____ 7 = 11

M. 14 ____ 7 = 7   N. 1 ____ 5 = 6   O. 2 ____ 2 = 4

P. 13 ____ 9 = 4   Q. 6 ____ 8 = 14   R. 9 ____ 4 = 13

S. 8 ____ 5 = 3   T. 5 ____ 5 = 10   U. 2 ____ 5 = 7

V. 13 ____ 9 = 4   W. 8 ____ 9 = 17   X. 11 ____ 7 = 4

Choose 3 number sentences. Prove they are true by drawing them here.

Tally the number of times you used each symbol.

Fill in the frequency table to match your tally chart.

Symbol	Number of Times
+	
−	

Symbol	Number of Times
+	
−	

Same Answer

Find the answer to each problem. Then, write one addition and one subtraction number sentence for the same answer.

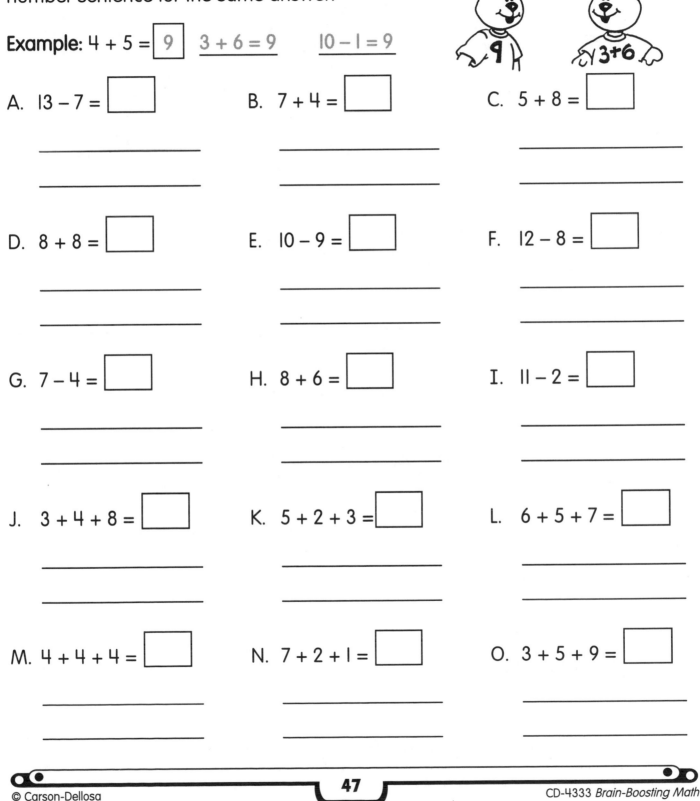

Example: $4 + 5 =$ ☐ 9 $3 + 6 = 9$ $10 - 1 = 9$

A. $13 - 7 =$ ☐

_____

_____

B. $7 + 4 =$ ☐

_____

_____

C. $5 + 8 =$ ☐

_____

_____

D. $8 + 8 =$ ☐

_____

_____

E. $10 - 9 =$ ☐

_____

_____

F. $12 - 8 =$ ☐

_____

_____

G. $7 - 4 =$ ☐

_____

_____

H. $8 + 6 =$ ☐

_____

_____

I. $11 - 2 =$ ☐

_____

_____

J. $3 + 4 + 8 =$ ☐

_____

_____

K. $5 + 2 + 3 =$ ☐

_____

_____

L. $6 + 5 + 7 =$ ☐

_____

_____

M. $4 + 4 + 4 =$ ☐

_____

_____

N. $7 + 2 + 1 =$ ☐

_____

_____

O. $3 + 5 + 9 =$ ☐

_____

_____

Homework Machine

Apply the rule on the handle to the numbers in the top row. Fill in the answers.

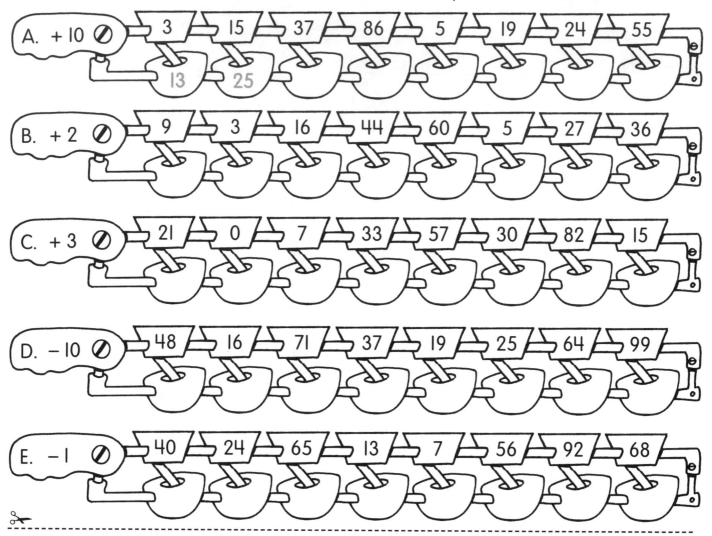

A. + 10   3   15   37   86   5   19   24   55
          13   25

B. + 2   9   3   16   44   60   5   27   36

C. + 3   21   0   7   33   57   30   82   15

D. – 10   48   16   71   37   19   25   64   99

E. – 1   40   24   65   13   7   56   92   68

✂ -

Write your own. Decide which rule the machine will run. Write it on the handle. Write the numbers to start in the top baskets. Write the answers in the boxes below the fold line. Fold under to hide. Trade with a partner.

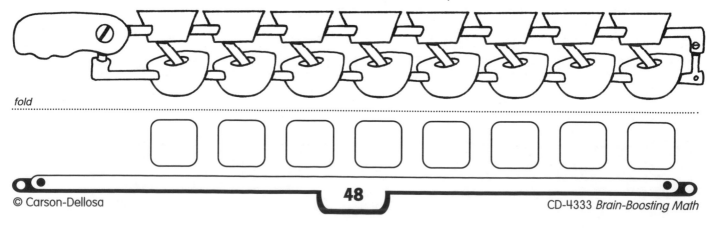

fold

Homework Machine (continued)

Find the rule for each homework machine. Fill in the missing numbers.

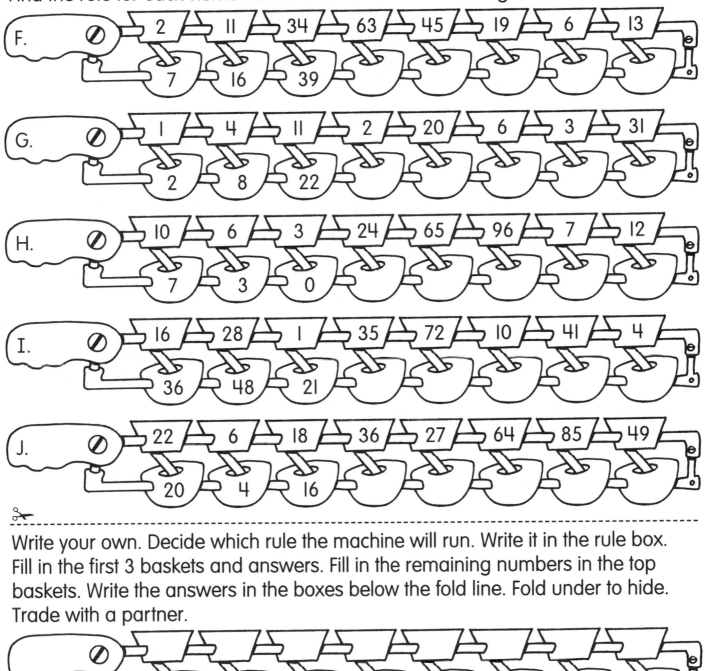

F. | 2 | 11 | 34 | 63 | 45 | 19 | 6 | 13 |
7 | 16 | 39 |

G. | 1 | 4 | 11 | 2 | 20 | 6 | 3 | 31 |
2 | 8 | 22 |

H. | 10 | 6 | 3 | 24 | 65 | 96 | 7 | 12 |
7 | 3 | 0 |

I. | 16 | 28 | 1 | 35 | 72 | 10 | 41 | 4 |
36 | 48 | 21 |

J. | 22 | 6 | 18 | 36 | 27 | 64 | 85 | 49 |
20 | 4 | 16 |

Write your own. Decide which rule the machine will run. Write it in the rule box. Fill in the first 3 baskets and answers. Fill in the remaining numbers in the top baskets. Write the answers in the boxes below the fold line. Fold under to hide. Trade with a partner.

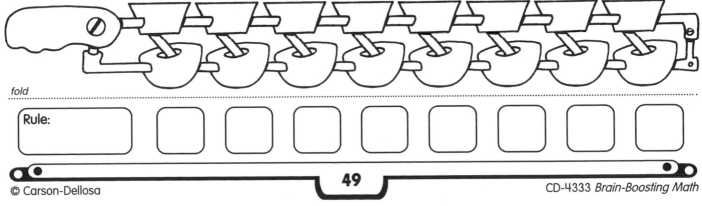

fold

Rule:

CD-4333 *Brain-Boosting Math*

Make That Number

Think of a number sentence whose **answer** is the given number. Write the number sentence. Think of more number sentences. Write each on a new line. Use addition, subtraction, and addition with 3 or more addends. If you need more space, use the back of this page or another sheet of paper.

A. **5**

_____   _____   _____

_____   _____   _____

_____   _____   _____

B. **12**

_____   _____   _____

_____   _____   _____

_____   _____   _____

C. **10**

_____   _____   _____

_____   _____   _____

_____   _____   _____

D. **9**

_____   _____   _____

_____   _____   _____

_____   _____   _____

Share your answers with a partner. Put a check next to the number sentences you both have. Circle the ones that only you have.

Name _____

Letter Math

addition with multiple addends

Use the table. Give each letter in the word a number value. Add the numbers to find the total value of the word.

Value Table

1	2	3	4	5	1	2	3	4	5
A	B	C	D	E	F	G	H	I	J
K	L	M	N	O	P	Q	R	S	T
U	V	W	X	Y	Z				

Example: CAT

$$\underset{3}{C} + \underset{1}{A} + \underset{5}{T} = \boxed{9}$$

1. add

_____

2. math

_____

3. square

_____

4. equal

_____

5. coins

_____

6. graph

_____

7. Find the value of this sentence: **Math is fun**.

_____

8. Write your name here. Find the value of your name.

_____

9. Write 4 words with a value of 7.

_____ _____ _____ _____

10. Write 4 words with a value greater than 15.

_____ _____ _____ _____

11. Write a sentence. Find the total value of the words in your sentence.

_____

 CD-4333 *Brain-Boosting Math*

What Number Am I?

Read the riddles. Write your answers as number words.

1 – one	2 – two	3 – three	4 – four	5 – five	6 – six
7 – seven	8 – eight	9 – nine	10 – ten	11 – eleven	12 – twelve
13 – thirteen	14 – fourteen	15 – fifteen	16 – sixteen	17 – seventeen	18 – eighteen

1. I am 5 less than 7. What number am I? _____

2. I am 2 more than 6. What number am I? _____

3. I am 3 fewer than 8. What number am I? _____

4. I am 4 more than 9. What number am I? _____

5. I am 13 minus 6. What number am I? _____

6. I am 1 more than 5. What number am I? _____

7. I am 6 less than 10. What number am I? _____

8. I am 8 subtract 6 add 2. What number am I? _____

9. I am 9 plus 4 minus 5. What number am I? _____

10. I am 4 add 5 add 2. What number am I? _____

11. I am 3 add 5 subtract 7. What number am I? _____

12. I am 12 subtract 6 add 8. What number am I? _____

What Is Missing?

Look at the number riddles.
Write the number that makes each equation true.

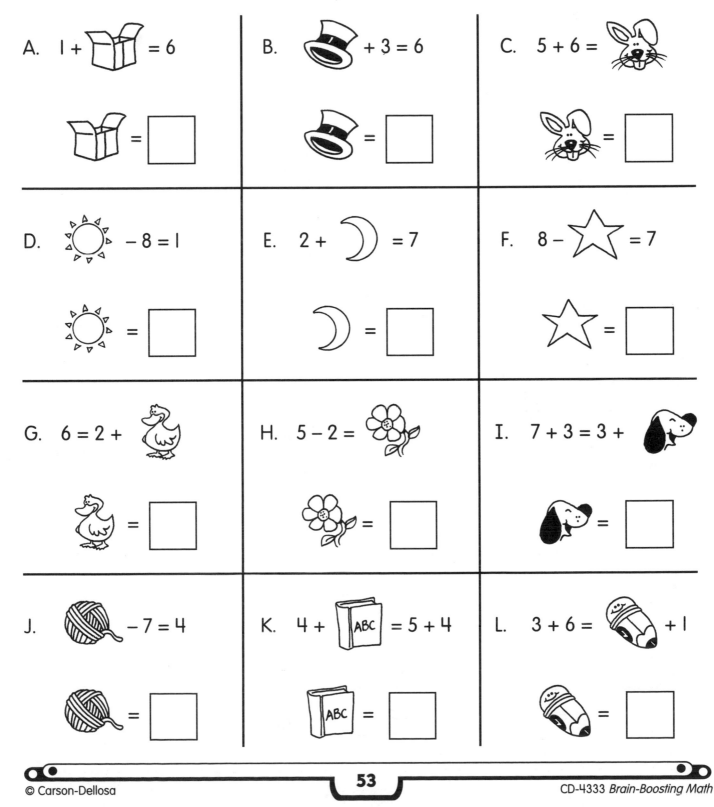

A. $1 + \boxed{} = 6$

$\boxed{} = \boxed{}$

B. $\boxed{} + 3 = 6$

$\boxed{} = \boxed{}$

C. $5 + 6 = \boxed{}$

$\boxed{} = \boxed{}$

D. $\boxed{} - 8 = 1$

$\boxed{} = \boxed{}$

E. $2 + \boxed{} = 7$

$\boxed{} = \boxed{}$

F. $8 - \boxed{} = 7$

$\boxed{} = \boxed{}$

G. $6 = 2 + \boxed{}$

$\boxed{} = \boxed{}$

H. $5 - 2 = \boxed{}$

$\boxed{} = \boxed{}$

I. $7 + 3 = 3 + \boxed{}$

$\boxed{} = \boxed{}$

J. $\boxed{} - 7 = 4$

$\boxed{} = \boxed{}$

K. $4 + \boxed{ABC} = 5 + 4$

$\boxed{ABC} = \boxed{}$

L. $3 + 6 = \boxed{} + 1$

$\boxed{} = \boxed{}$

CD-4333 *Brain-Boosting Math*

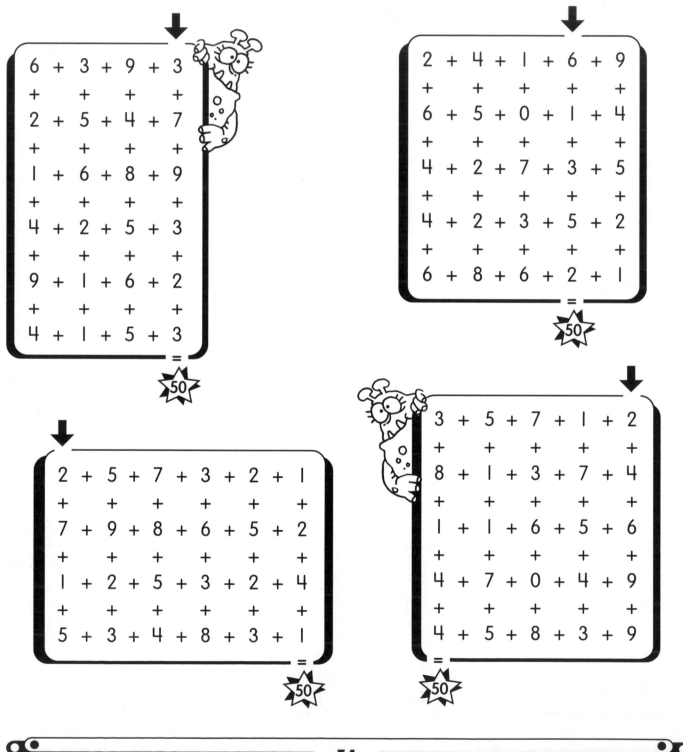

Hidden Pathways

addition/problem solving

Find each hidden pathway. Begin at the arrow. Add your way to 50 in the bottom row. You may only move up, down, or across—not diagonally. DO NOT cross your path. The sum of the numbers in your path must be exactly 50.

6 + 3 + 9 + 3
+   +   +   +
2 + 5 + 4 + 7
+   +   +   +
1 + 6 + 8 + 9
+   +   +   +
4 + 2 + 5 + 3
+   +   +   +
9 + 1 + 6 + 2
+   +   +   +
4 + 1 + 5 + 3
= 50

2 + 4 + 1 + 6 + 9
+   +   +   +   +
6 + 5 + 0 + 1 + 4
+   +   +   +   +
4 + 2 + 7 + 3 + 5
+   +   +   +   +
4 + 2 + 3 + 5 + 2
+   +   +   +   +
6 + 8 + 6 + 2 + 1
= 50

2 + 5 + 7 + 3 + 2 + 1
+   +   +   +   +   +
7 + 9 + 8 + 6 + 5 + 2
+   +   +   +   +   +
1 + 2 + 5 + 3 + 2 + 4
+   +   +   +   +   +
5 + 3 + 4 + 8 + 3 + 1
= 50

3 + 5 + 7 + 1 + 2
+   +   +   +   +
8 + 1 + 3 + 7 + 4
+   +   +   +   +
1 + 1 + 6 + 5 + 6
+   +   +   +   +
4 + 7 + 0 + 4 + 9
+   +   +   +   +
4 + 5 + 8 + 3 + 9
= 50

CD-4333 *Brain-Boosting Math*

Roman Numerals

Roman numerals/place value/addition and subtraction

Fill in the chart. In the fourth column, write a number sentence whose answer is the number. In the last column, rewrite it using Roman numerals.

I = 1   V = 5
X = 10

Picture Form	Number	Roman Numeral	Number Sentence	Number Sentence in Roman Numerals
•	I	I	3 – 2 = 1	III – II = I
• •				
• • •				
• • • •				
• • • • •				
• • • • • •				
• • • • • • •				
• • • • • • • •				
• • • • • • • • •				
I				
I •				
I • •				
I • • •				
I • • • •				
I • • • • •				
I • • • • • •				
II • • •				
III • • • • • •				

Name _____

Using Roman Numerals

Roman numerals

Read the creature facts. Underline the Roman numerals.
Write each Roman numeral in standard form in the box.

I = 1   V = 5   X = 10   L = 50   C = 100

1. One enormous dinosaur had a brain that weighed about the same as III pencils.

2. A grasshopper has VI legs.

3. The Madagascar hissing cockroach is about VIII centimeters long.

4. The crow, like many other birds, has IV toes on each foot.

5. The African ostrich can weigh CCLX pounds.

6. A humpback whale's tail can be XVIII feet across.

7. The largest baleen whales grow to XCIX feet long.

8. The United States has CCXI species of amphibians.

9. A tiger can eat up to LXV pounds of meat at one time.

10. The giraffe is the tallest land animal. It grows as tall as XIX feet.

11. The ostrich cannot fly but can run up to XLV miles per hour.

12. The emperor penguin weighs up to LXXXV pounds.

CD-4333 *Brain-Boosting Math*

Up in the Air

Solve.

A.
$$83$$
$$+ 15$$

B.
$$27$$
$$+ 42$$

C.
$$14$$
$$+ 34$$

D.
$$62$$
$$+ 26$$

E.
$$15$$
$$+ 12$$

F. $51 + 37 =$

G. $12 + 14 =$

H. $40 + 33 =$

I.
$$32$$
$$+ 43$$

J.
$$73$$
$$+ 23$$

K.
$$41$$
$$+ 17$$

L.
$$26$$
$$+ 12$$

M.
$$54$$
$$+ 22$$

N. $39 + 10 =$

O. $21 + 41 =$

P. $13 + 65 =$

Color the balloons:

red	if even + even = even
green	if even + even = odd
blue	if odd + even = odd or even + odd = odd
brown	if odd + even = even or even + odd = even
yellow	if odd + odd = even
orange	if odd + odd = odd

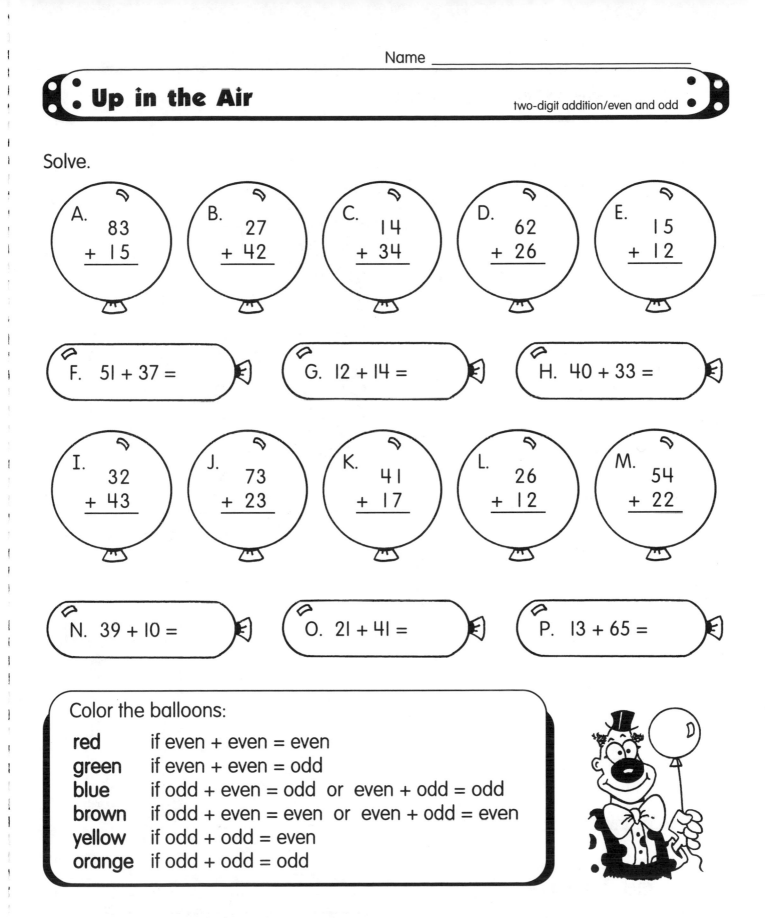

What did you notice when you colored the balloons? Share your ideas.

Swatting Flies

two-digit subtraction, no regrouping/grid coordinates

Use your answers to swat at the flies. Move across the number of the tens digit and up the number of the ones digit. Draw an **X** on the space where you land.

Example:

$$\begin{array}{r} 58 \\ -\ 12 \\ \hline 46 \end{array}$$

On the grid, go over 4 and up 6.

A.
$$\begin{array}{r} 36 \\ -\ 25 \\ \hline \end{array}$$

B.
$$\begin{array}{r} 48 \\ -\ 16 \\ \hline \end{array}$$

C.
$$\begin{array}{r} 55 \\ -\ 42 \\ \hline \end{array}$$

D.
$$\begin{array}{r} 63 \\ -\ 41 \\ \hline \end{array}$$

E.
$$\begin{array}{r} 37 \\ -\ 21 \\ \hline \end{array}$$

F.
$$\begin{array}{r} 26 \\ -\ \ 5 \\ \hline \end{array}$$

G.
$$\begin{array}{r} 47 \\ -\ 32 \\ \hline \end{array}$$

H.
$$\begin{array}{r} 33 \\ -\ 21 \\ \hline \end{array}$$

I.
$$\begin{array}{r} 48 \\ -\ 22 \\ \hline \end{array}$$

J.
$$\begin{array}{r} 57 \\ -\ 23 \\ \hline \end{array}$$

K.
$$\begin{array}{r} 99 \\ -\ 38 \\ \hline \end{array}$$

L.
$$\begin{array}{r} 87 \\ -\ 24 \\ \hline \end{array}$$

M.
$$\begin{array}{r} 77 \\ -\ 36 \\ \hline \end{array}$$

N.
$$\begin{array}{r} 88 \\ -\ 35 \\ \hline \end{array}$$

O.
$$\begin{array}{r} 86 \\ -\ 41 \\ \hline \end{array}$$

P.
$$\begin{array}{r} 78 \\ -\ 13 \\ \hline \end{array}$$

Q. How many flies did you catch? _____

R. How many answers missed? _____

S. Write subtraction problems to help you catch 3 more flies.

Addition Steps

addition and subtraction, no regrouping

Climb your way to the top! Add adjacent numbers. Write each sum in the box above and between the two numbers. Keep adding until you reach the top.

A.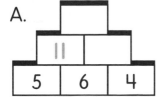

B.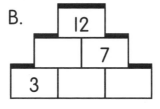

C.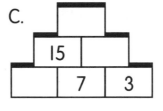

D.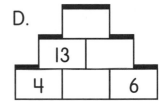

E.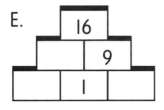

F.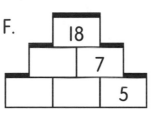

G.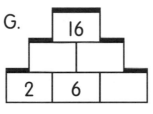

H.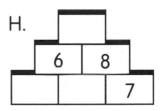

I.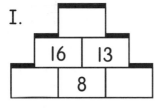

J.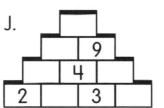

K.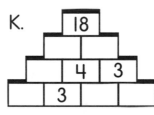

L.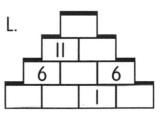

Write your own. Fill in the bottom row. Add to the top. Check your answers with a calculator.

Fill in the bottom row. Leave the other boxes blank. Fold to hide your answers. Trade with a friend.

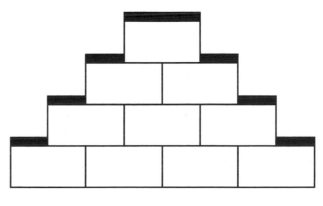

CD-4333 *Brain-Boosting Math*

Fire Safety

Add or subtract. Write the answers from each row in order from least to greatest on the lines. Then, write the letter next to the problem in the box to find an important rule of fire safety.

```
    36          99          54          32
  + 42        - 26        - 12        + 47
  O           T           S           P
```

```
    84          56          21          65
  - 31        - 43        + 18        - 22
  P           D           R           O
```

```
    30          26          84
  + 69        + 42        - 11
  D           A           N
```

```
    86          43          16          93
  - 56        + 15        + 13        - 11
  O           L           R           L
```

Dot-to-Dot

two-digit addition and subtraction, no regrouping/sequencing

Solve. Connect the dots in order from least to greatest.

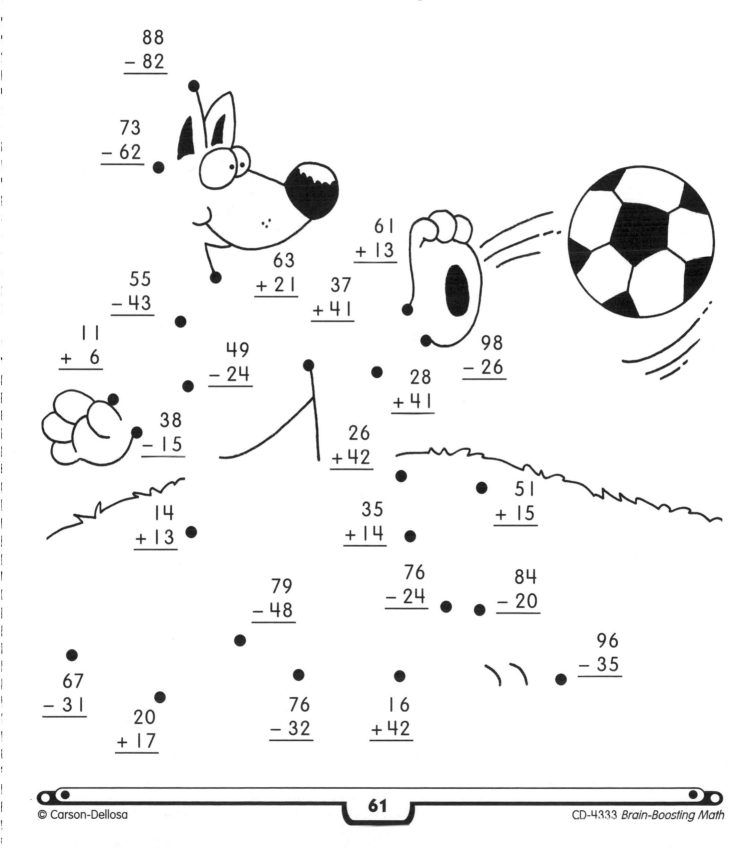

$$\begin{array}{r} 88 \\ -82 \\ \hline \end{array}$$

$$\begin{array}{r} 73 \\ -62 \\ \hline \end{array}$$

$$\begin{array}{r} 55 \\ -43 \\ \hline \end{array}$$

$$\begin{array}{r} 11 \\ +6 \\ \hline \end{array}$$

$$\begin{array}{r} 63 \\ +21 \\ \hline \end{array}$$

$$\begin{array}{r} 49 \\ -24 \\ \hline \end{array}$$

$$\begin{array}{r} 38 \\ -15 \\ \hline \end{array}$$

$$\begin{array}{r} 37 \\ +41 \\ \hline \end{array}$$

$$\begin{array}{r} 61 \\ +13 \\ \hline \end{array}$$

$$\begin{array}{r} 98 \\ -26 \\ \hline \end{array}$$

$$\begin{array}{r} 28 \\ +41 \\ \hline \end{array}$$

$$\begin{array}{r} 26 \\ +42 \\ \hline \end{array}$$

$$\begin{array}{r} 14 \\ +13 \\ \hline \end{array}$$

$$\begin{array}{r} 35 \\ +14 \\ \hline \end{array}$$

$$\begin{array}{r} 51 \\ +15 \\ \hline \end{array}$$

$$\begin{array}{r} 79 \\ -48 \\ \hline \end{array}$$

$$\begin{array}{r} 76 \\ -24 \\ \hline \end{array}$$

$$\begin{array}{r} 84 \\ -20 \\ \hline \end{array}$$

$$\begin{array}{r} 96 \\ -35 \\ \hline \end{array}$$

$$\begin{array}{r} 67 \\ -31 \\ \hline \end{array}$$

$$\begin{array}{r} 20 \\ +17 \\ \hline \end{array}$$

$$\begin{array}{r} 76 \\ -32 \\ \hline \end{array}$$

$$\begin{array}{r} 16 \\ +42 \\ \hline \end{array}$$

CD-4333 *Brain-Boosting Math*

Start Where You Left Off

addition and subtraction

Solve. Use each answer to start the next problem.

A. [ ]
+ 2 3

B. [ ]
+ 2 1

C. [ ]
− 5 3

D. [ ]
− 2 1

E. [ ]
+ 4 4

F. [ ]
− 1 7

G. [ ]
+ 4 0

H. [ ]
− 7 1

I. [ ]
+ 3 4

J. [ ]
+ 2 2

K. [ ]
+ 2 1

L. [ ]
− 5 6

M. [ ]
− 1 2

N. [ ]
+ 7 7

O. [ ]
− 8 5

P. [ ]
+ 3 2

Q. [ ]
− 1 3

R. [ ]
+ 6 8

S. [ ]
− 3 2

T. [ ]
− 1 5

U. [ ]
− 3 0

V. [ ]
− 2 2

What is your final answer?
If it is not 0, go back
and check your work!

CD-4333 *Brain-Boosting Math*

Ant Farm

problem solving/two-digit addition and subtraction, no regrouping

Use the information below to answer the questions.

Yurelli, 24 ants   Talia, 46 ants   Sousi, 33 ants   Kalae, 12 ants

1. How many ants do Kalae and Talia have all together?

_____

2. How many more ants does Sousi have than Kalae?

_____

3. What is the total number of ants in Yurelli's, Sousi's, and Kalae's ant farms?

_____

4. If 9 of Kalae's ants get away, how many ants will she have?

_____

5. Talia looked in her ant farm and saw only 35 ants. How many ants got away?

6. Talia decided to buy a vial of 50 more ants. How many does she have now?

_____

7. Yurelli also bought a vial of 50 ants. How many will she have in the ant farm when she puts them in?

_____

8. While Yurelli was putting the ants in, 12 got away. How many ants are in Yurelli's ant farm now?

_____

9. Now who has more ants, Yurelli or Talia? How many more?

CD-4333 *Brain-Boosting Math*

Missing Digits

problem solving/two-digit addition and subtraction, no regrouping

Name _____

Add or subtract. Find the missing digits.

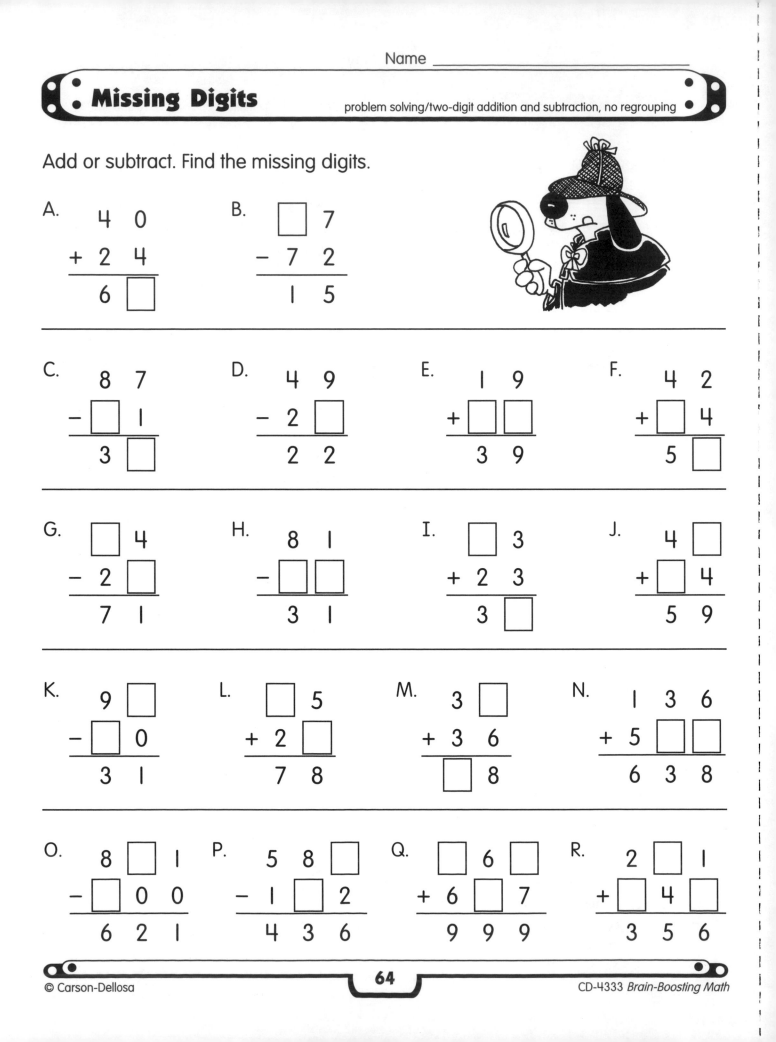

A.
```
   4 0
 + 2 4
 ------
   6 ☐
```

B.
```
   ☐ 7
 - 7 2
 ------
   1 5
```

C.
```
   8 7
 - ☐ 1
 ------
   3 ☐
```

D.
```
   4 9
 - 2 ☐
 ------
   2 2
```

E.
```
   1 9
 + ☐ ☐
 ------
   3 9
```

F.
```
   4 2
 + ☐ 4
 ------
   5 ☐
```

G.
```
   ☐ 4
 - 2 ☐
 ------
   7 1
```

H.
```
   8 1
 - ☐ ☐
 ------
   3 1
```

I.
```
   ☐ 3
 + 2 3
 ------
   3 ☐
```

J.
```
   4 ☐
 + ☐ 4
 ------
   5 9
```

K.
```
   9 ☐
 - ☐ 0
 ------
   3 1
```

L.
```
   ☐ 5
 + 2 ☐
 ------
   7 8
```

M.
```
   3 ☐
 + 3 6
 ------
   ☐ 8
```

N.
```
   1 3 6
 + 5 ☐ ☐
 --------
   6 3 8
```

O.
```
   8 ☐ 1
 - ☐ 0 0
 --------
   6 2 1
```

P.
```
   5 8 ☐
 - 1 ☐ 2
 --------
   4 3 6
```

Q.
```
   ☐ 6 ☐
 + 6 ☐ 7
 --------
   9 9 9
```

R.
```
   2 ☐ 1
 + ☐ 4 ☐
 --------
   3 5 6
```

Missing Digits (continued)

Make your own 2-digit addition and subtraction problems (no regrouping).
Check for accuracy with a calculator.

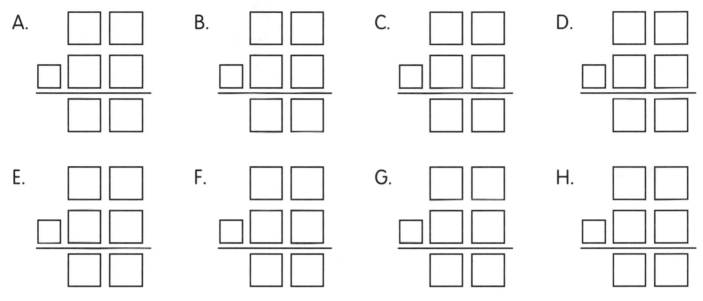

A.   B.   C.   D.

E.   F.   G.   H.

Copy your problems into the boxes below. Leave the shaded boxes blank.
Fold the paper back along the fold line. Trade with a friend.

fold

Add or subtract. Find the missing digits. When you are done, open the page and
check your answers.

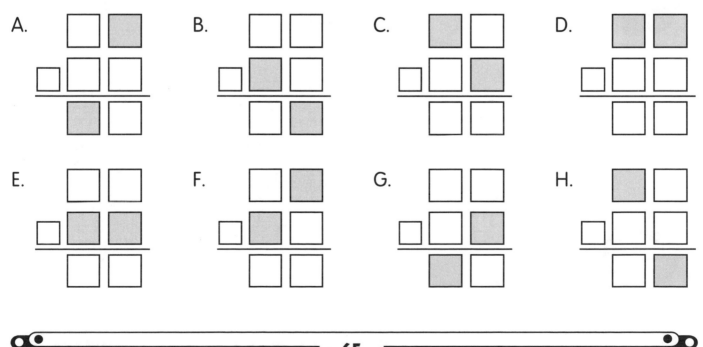

A.   B.   C.   D.

E.   F.   G.   H.

CD-4333 *Brain-Boosting Math*

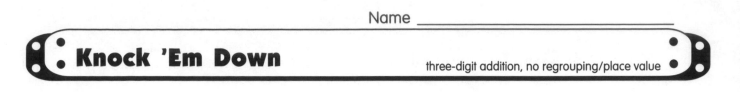

Knock 'Em Down

three-digit addition, no regrouping/place value

Solve. For each set, color the pins that go with the ball.

A.

even sums

$$512 + 236$$ $$471 + 113$$ $$284 + 305$$ $$322 + 154$$

B.

< 400

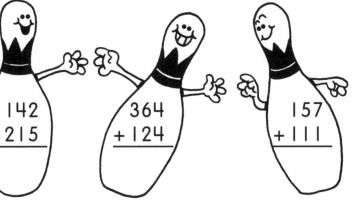

$$142 + 215$$ $$364 + 124$$ $$157 + 111$$ $$407 + 452$$

C.

9 in ones place

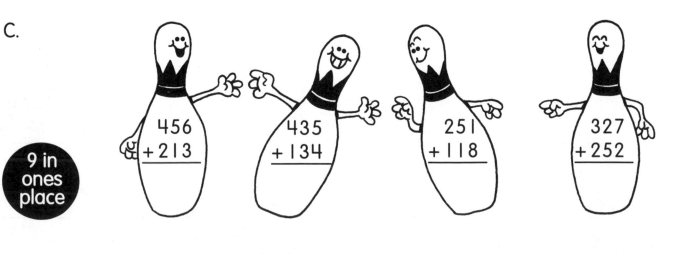

$$456 + 213$$ $$435 + 134$$ $$251 + 118$$ $$327 + 252$$

CD-4333 *Brain-Boosting Math*

Name _____

The world's largest penguin weighs up to 88 pounds. The second largest weighs about half as much. Both birds stand about 3 feet tall. Solve the problems to find the names of these penguins. Write the correct letter above each answer below.

P 678
− 543

O 467
− 114

N 775
− 321

I 534
− 521

P 988
− 233

P 968
− 236

R 593
− 152

I 591
− 441

G 549
− 306

R 396
− 251

K 284
− 81

E 178
− 154

E 884
− 364

N 728
− 518

M 937
− 215

N 726
− 215

N 346
− 145

G 257
− 114

E 815
− 701

U 668
− 316

J 634
− 121

G 695
− 263

I 854
− 342

E 684
− 523

N 258
− 127

The largest penguin is the:

___ ___ ___ ___ ___ ___ ___
161 722 135 520 441 353 145

The second largest penguin is the:

___ ___ ___ ___
203 13 210 432

___ ___ ___ ___ ___ ___ ___
732 24 454 143 352 150 511

___ ___ ___ ___ ___ ___ ___
755 114 201 243 513 512 131

CD-4333 *Brain-Boosting Math*

Roofing Houses

Rewrite the problems in vertical form. Solve.

A. 461 + 502

```
  461
+ 502
```

B. 768 – 541

C. 859 – 735

D. 447 + 241

E. 966 – 341

F. 197 + 202

G. 314 + 522

H. 273 – 250

I. 538 – 215

J. 724 – 412

K. 614 + 113

L. 408 + 120

Use the key to color the houses:

If the answer is even, trace the house with red.
If the answer is odd, trace the house with blue.
If the answer is > 200, color the house yellow.
If the answer has a 2 in the tens place, color the roof green.

Number Venn

three-digit addition and subtraction, no regrouping/Venn diagram

Put these numbers in the Venn diagram:

| 143 | 549 | 471 | 242 | 843 | 647 | 584 | 624 | 148 | 231 | 628 |

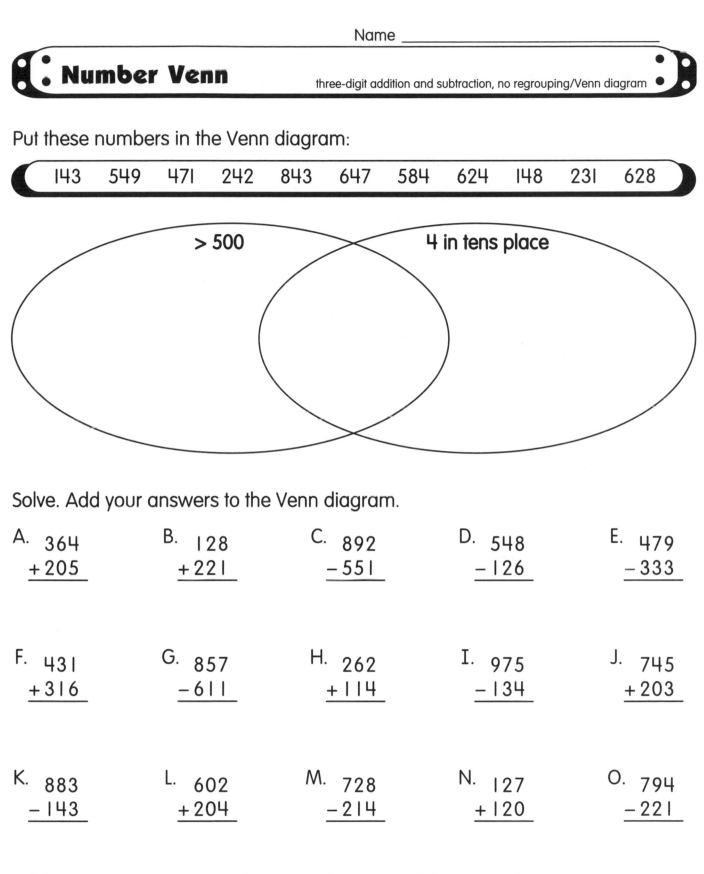

> 500

4 in tens place

Solve. Add your answers to the Venn diagram.

A. 364
  + 205

B. 128
  + 221

C. 892
  − 551

D. 548
  − 126

E. 479
  − 333

F. 431
  + 316

G. 857
  − 611

H. 262
  + 114

I. 975
  − 134

J. 745
  + 203

K. 883
  − 143

L. 602
  + 204

M. 728
  − 214

N. 127
  + 120

O. 794
  − 221

Add at least one more number to each section of the Venn diagram.
Circle your added numbers. Don't forget about the outside set!

CD-4333 *Brain-Boosting Math*

Pull It Apart

Write out each problem in word form. Add the ones.
Add the tens. Regroup. Write the answer in number form.

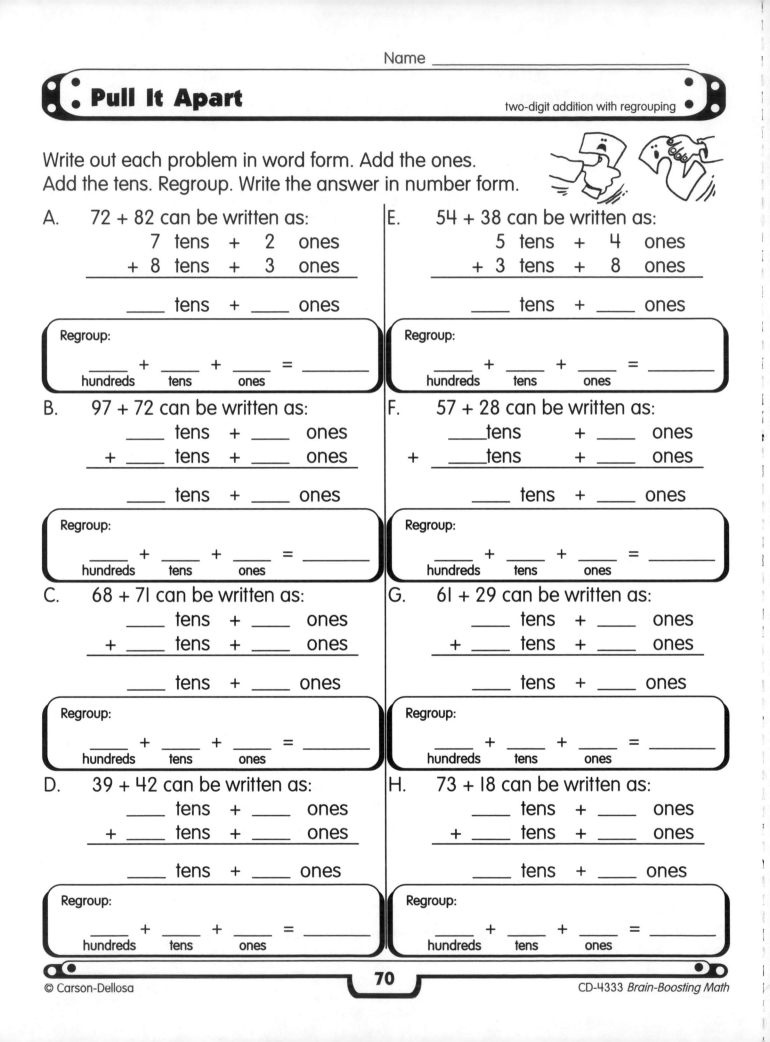

A.   72 + 82 can be written as:

$$7 \text{ tens } + \ 2 \text{ ones}$$
$$+ \ 8 \text{ tens } + \ 3 \text{ ones}$$

____ tens + ____ ones

Regroup:

____ + ____ + ____ = _____
hundreds   tens   ones

B.   97 + 72 can be written as:

____ tens + ____ ones
+ ____ tens + ____ ones

____ tens + ____ ones

Regroup:

____ + ____ + ____ = _____
hundreds   tens   ones

C.   68 + 71 can be written as:

____ tens + ____ ones
+ ____ tens + ____ ones

____ tens + ____ ones

Regroup:

____ + ____ + ____ = _____
hundreds   tens   ones

D.   39 + 42 can be written as:

____ tens + ____ ones
+ ____ tens + ____ ones

____ tens + ____ ones

Regroup:

____ + ____ + ____ = _____
hundreds   tens   ones

E.   54 + 38 can be written as:

$$5 \text{ tens } + \ 4 \text{ ones}$$
$$+ \ 3 \text{ tens } + \ 8 \text{ ones}$$

____ tens + ____ ones

Regroup:

____ + ____ + ____ = _____
hundreds   tens   ones

F.   57 + 28 can be written as:

____ tens + ____ ones
+ ____ tens + ____ ones

____ tens + ____ ones

Regroup:

____ + ____ + ____ = _____
hundreds   tens   ones

G.   61 + 29 can be written as:

____ tens + ____ ones
+ ____ tens + ____ ones

____ tens + ____ ones

Regroup:

____ + ____ + ____ = _____
hundreds   tens   ones

H.   73 + 18 can be written as:

____ tens + ____ ones
+ ____ tens + ____ ones

____ tens + ____ ones

Regroup:

____ + ____ + ____ = _____
hundreds   tens   ones

CD-4333 *Brain-Boosting Math*

Old Bug

two-digit addition with regrouping/even and odd/sequencing

Solve.
Circle the odd answers with blue.
Circle the even answers with red.

E 12
    +29

S 53
    +74

A 53
    +65

H 96
    +90

I 83
    +64

C 72
    +90

O 28
    + 2

P 95
    +72

G 82
    +99

K 26
    +68

S 59
    +88

P 38
    +89

C 48
    +18

O 75
    +39

R 93
    +17

T 66
    +49

C 15
    + 7

Scientists found a fossil of a bug that is older than the dinosaurs. It was found in Ohio. Write the even answers on the lines below in order from smallest to largest. Write the correct letter above each number to find out what ancient bug is still with us today.

CD-4333 *Brain-Boosting Math*

Picture It

Start with 1. Write the numbers from 1 to 100 in the chart.

1							8		
		13							
									100

Solve. Shade in your answers in the chart to reveal a picture.

A. $\begin{array}{r} 58 \\ +27 \\ \hline \end{array}$ B. $\begin{array}{r} 46 \\ +27 \\ \hline \end{array}$ C. $\begin{array}{r} 28 \\ +27 \\ \hline \end{array}$ D. $\begin{array}{r} 14 \\ +\ 9 \\ \hline \end{array}$ E. $\begin{array}{r} 17 \\ +19 \\ \hline \end{array}$ F. $\begin{array}{r} 78 \\ +\ 9 \\ \hline \end{array}$ G. $\begin{array}{r} 19 \\ +59 \\ \hline \end{array}$ H. $\begin{array}{r} 34 \\ +35 \\ \hline \end{array}$

I. $\begin{array}{r} 18 \\ +15 \\ \hline \end{array}$ J. $\begin{array}{r} 18 \\ +68 \\ \hline \end{array}$ K. $\begin{array}{r} 38 \\ +\ 8 \\ \hline \end{array}$ L. $\begin{array}{r} 39 \\ +17 \\ \hline \end{array}$ M. $\begin{array}{r} 19 \\ +\ 9 \\ \hline \end{array}$ N. $\begin{array}{r} 19 \\ +19 \\ \hline \end{array}$ O. $\begin{array}{r} 35 \\ +27 \\ \hline \end{array}$ P. $\begin{array}{r} 49 \\ +35 \\ \hline \end{array}$

Information

Use the frequency tables to answer the questions.

What color are your eyes?	
Color	Number of Students
blue	8
brown	12
green	2
other	1

What kind of pet do you have?	
Pet	Number of Houses
bird	3
cat	8
dog	10
fish	5
other	6

What is your favorite fruit?	
Fruit	Number of Students
apple	8
banana	8
grape	6
orange	4
other	5

1. How many more students have brown eyes than blue eyes?

   _____

2. What is the total number of students with green or blue eyes?

   _____

3. How many more houses have fish than birds?

   _____

4. How many more houses have dogs than fish?

   _____

5. What is the total number of houses with cats or dogs?

   _____

6. How many more students prefer grapes than oranges?

   _____

7. How many students prefer apples compared to those who like bananas?

   _____

8. What is the total number of students who prefer apples or bananas?

   _____

CD-4333 *Brain-Boosting Math*

Pictograph

Margie's class made a frequency table to show what the second graders did during choice time. Use the table to make a pictograph below.

Activity	Number of Students
read	18
finish work	6
dice math	24
color	12
clean desk	6
science project	18

Draw 1 ☺ for every 2 students.

Activity	Number of Students
read	
finish work	
dice math	
color	
clean desk	
science project	

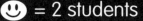

☺ = 2 students

1. If 10 students made an art project, how many faces would you make? _____

2. If each ☺ = 2 students, how would you show 1 student? _____   9 students? _____

3. Circle **T** for true or **F** for false.

    T   F   More students chose dice math than coloring.
    T   F   An equal number of students read as did the science project.
    T   F   Fewer students colored than cleaned desks.
    T   F   Ten more students finished work than read.

Use the information in the frequency table to make another graph on the back of this page. This time, draw one ☺ for every 3 students.

Cookie Count

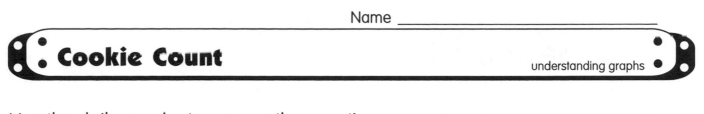

Use the daily graphs to answer the questions.

Day One	
Name	Cookies Made
Bill	
Jill	
Phil	
Will	

⬭ = 4 cookies

Day Two	
Name	Cookies Made
Bill	
Jill	
Phil	
Will	

⬭ = 4 cookies

1. Who made the most cookies on Day One? _____

   How many cookies? _____

2. Did Bill make more cookies on Day One or Two? _____

   How many more did he make? _____

3. Who made the most cookies total on Days One and Two? _____

   How many in all? _____

4. What is the total number of cookies made on Day Two? _____

5. Make a graph for Day Three using the information given.

Day Three	
Name	Cookies Made
Bill	
Jill	
Phil	
Will	

⬭ = 4 cookies

- Will made 8 fewer than on Day Two.

- Jill made 4 more than on Day One.

- Phil made the same number as on Day One.

- Bill made 4 fewer than Phil made.

6. Redo the graph for Day One on the back of this page. Let ⬭ = 2 cookies.
   Is the information any different? How does the new graph look different?

How Old Are You?

Mrs. Pat's class made a table to show the ages of the students.

How Old Are You?

Name	Age	Name	Age	Name	Age	Name	Age
Ian	6	Obed	7	Sixto	7	Meg	6
Omarha	8	Aidaly	7	Mikaela	7	Shawnice	7
Danielle	7	Rebecca	7	Esbeide	6	Willie	8
Nina	7	Arthur	6	Jordan	7	Brett	6
Melina	7	Liana	7				

1. Use the information from the table above to fill in the tally chart.

Age	Number of Students
6	
7	
8	

2. Draw an **X** on the frequency table that matches your tally chart.

Age	Number of Students	Age	Number of Students	Age	Number of Students
6	5	6	5	6	6
7	10	7	11	7	12
8	3	8	2	8	1

3. Use the frequency table to make a graph on another sheet of paper.

4. Look at the information. Circle **T** for true or **F** for false.

   T   F   Eleven students are 7 years old.

   T   F   The same number are 8 as 7.

   T   F   Fewer students are 8 than 6.

   T   F   Three more students are 6 than 8.

   T   F   Most students are 7.

   T   F   Fewer students are 7 than 6.

Simple Machines

Ryan's class is studying simple machines. Ryan counted the number of simple machines he saw in a day. He recorded the results in this tally chart.

Simple Machine	Number Seen	Simple Machine	Number Seen
inclined plane	‖‖‖ ‖‖‖ ‖‖‖‖	screw	‖‖‖ ‖‖‖ ‖
lever	‖‖‖ ‖‖‖ ‖‖	wedge	‖‖‖ ‖‖‖‖
pulley	‖‖‖ ‖‖‖‖	wheel and axle	‖‖‖ ‖‖‖ ‖‖‖ ‖

Complete the graph using the information from the tally chart. Color 1 box for each machine Ryan saw. Use a different color for each type of machine.

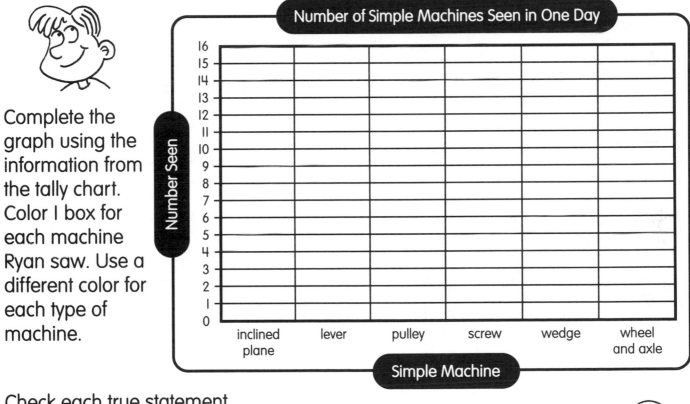

Number of Simple Machines Seen in One Day

Number Seen: 16 15 14 13 12 11 10 9 8 7 6 5 4 3 2 1 0

inclined plane · lever · pulley · screw · wedge · wheel and axle

Simple Machine

Check each true statement.

____ The wheel and axle was found most often.

____ Ryan found the lever the fewest number of times.

____ Screws were found more often than inclined planes.

____ Pulleys and wedges were found an equal number of times.

Write 1 true statement of your own about the data.

_____

Name _____

Look at the pictures. Fill in the blanks. Write each fraction under the correct letter.

1. Total number of equal parts: __5__

   a. white = _2_ out of _5_

   b. dotted = ___ out of ___

   c. shaded = ___ out of ___

   d. white + dotted = ___ out of ___

a	b	c	d
2			
5			

2. Total number of equal parts: _____

   a. dotted = ___ out of ___

   b. striped = ___ out of ___

   c. stars = ___ out of ___

   d. stars + striped = ___ out of ___

a	b	c	d

3. Total number of equal parts: _____

   a. hearts = ___ out of ___

   b. striped = ___ out of ___

   c. white = ___ out of ___

   d. hearts + white = ___ out of ___

a	b	c	d

4. Total number of equal parts: _____

   a. hearts = ___ out of ___

   b. stars = ___ out of ___

   c. shaded = ___ out of ___

   d. striped = ___ out of ___

   e. white = ___ out of ___

   f. striped + hearts = ___ out of ___

   g. white + hearts + stars = ___ out of ___

a	b	c	d

e	f	g

CD-4333 *Brain-Boosting Math*

Name _____

Coloring Fractions

Follow the directions. Write the fractions.

Color the candies in the cookie. Color I green.
Color I red. Color 3 yellow. Color 2 blue.

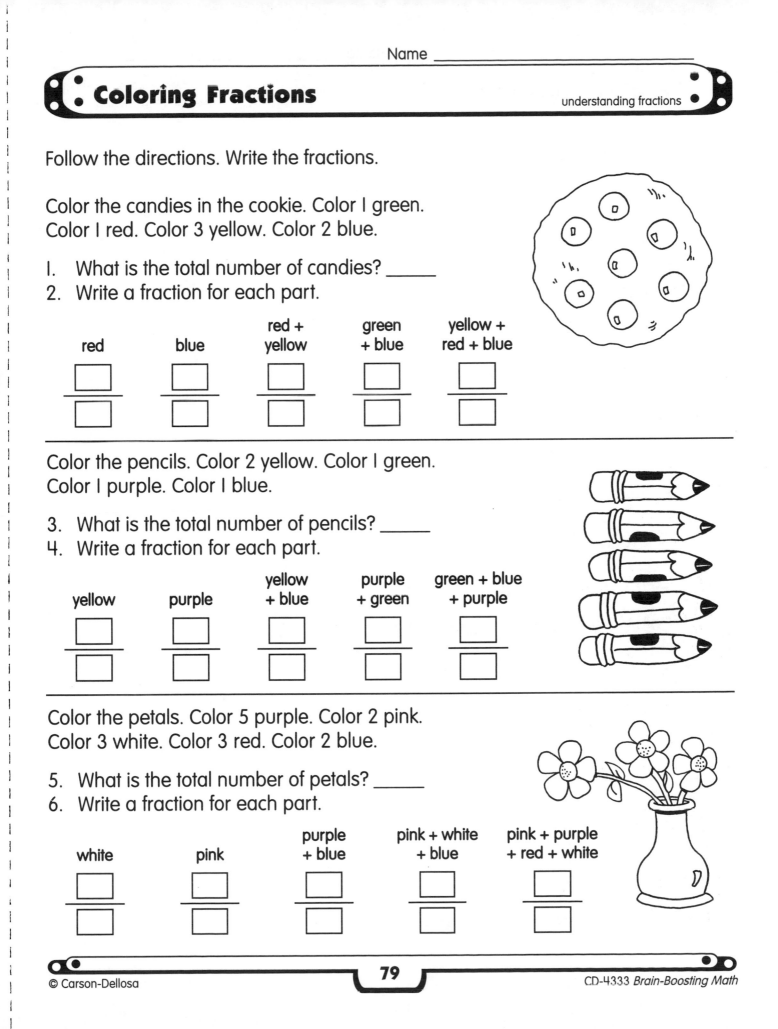

1. What is the total number of candies? _____
2. Write a fraction for each part.

red	blue	red + yellow	green + blue	yellow + red + blue
☐	☐	☐	☐	☐
☐	☐	☐	☐	☐

Color the pencils. Color 2 yellow. Color I green.
Color I purple. Color I blue.

3. What is the total number of pencils? _____
4. Write a fraction for each part.

yellow	purple	yellow + blue	purple + green	green + blue + purple
☐	☐	☐	☐	☐
☐	☐	☐	☐	☐

Color the petals. Color 5 purple. Color 2 pink.
Color 3 white. Color 3 red. Color 2 blue.

5. What is the total number of petals? _____
6. Write a fraction for each part.

white	pink	purple + blue	pink + white + blue	pink + purple + red + white
☐	☐	☐	☐	☐
☐	☐	☐	☐	☐

Fraction Draw

Draw the pictures. Write the fraction. Color.

1. Draw 2 squares.

    Color 1 out of 2 or _____ red.

2. Draw 5 circles.

    Color 3 out of 5 or _____ yellow.

    Color 1 out of 5 or _____ green.

3. Draw 4 ovals.

    Color 1 out of 4 or _____ orange.

    Color 2 out of 4 or _____ blue.

4. Draw 6 rectangles.

    Color 4 out of 6 or _____ black.

    Color 1 out of 6 or _____ yellow.

5. Draw 3 ovals.

    Color 1 out of 3 or _____ green.

    Color 2 out of 3 or _____ purple.

6. Draw 9 circles.

    Color 3 out of 9 or _____ yellow.

    Color 4 out of 9 or _____ orange.

    Color 1 out of 9 or _____ green.

Fraction Twins

Fractions can be used to describe part of a whole or part of a set.

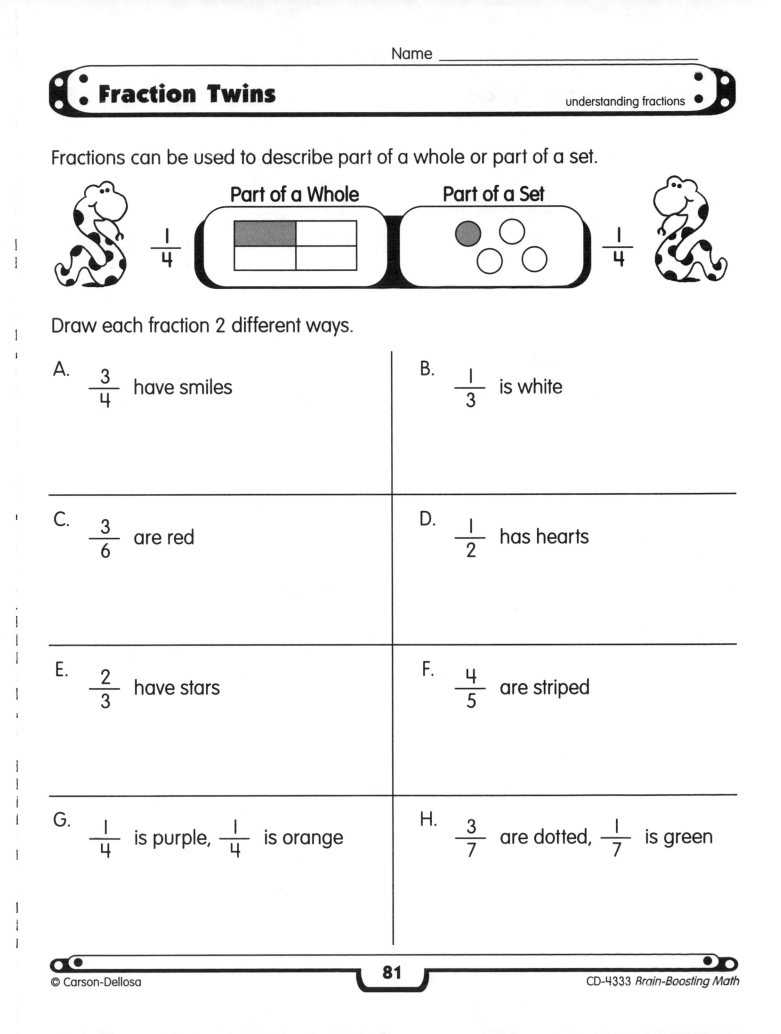

Part of a Whole   **Part of a Set**

$\frac{1}{4}$ $\frac{1}{4}$

Draw each fraction 2 different ways.

A. $\frac{3}{4}$ have smiles

B. $\frac{1}{3}$ is white

C. $\frac{3}{6}$ are red

D. $\frac{1}{2}$ has hearts

E. $\frac{2}{3}$ have stars

F. $\frac{4}{5}$ are striped

G. $\frac{1}{4}$ is purple, $\frac{1}{4}$ is orange

H. $\frac{3}{7}$ are dotted, $\frac{1}{7}$ is green

The Biggest Piece

making and comparing fractions

Use different colors to show who ate each part. Circle the correct answers.

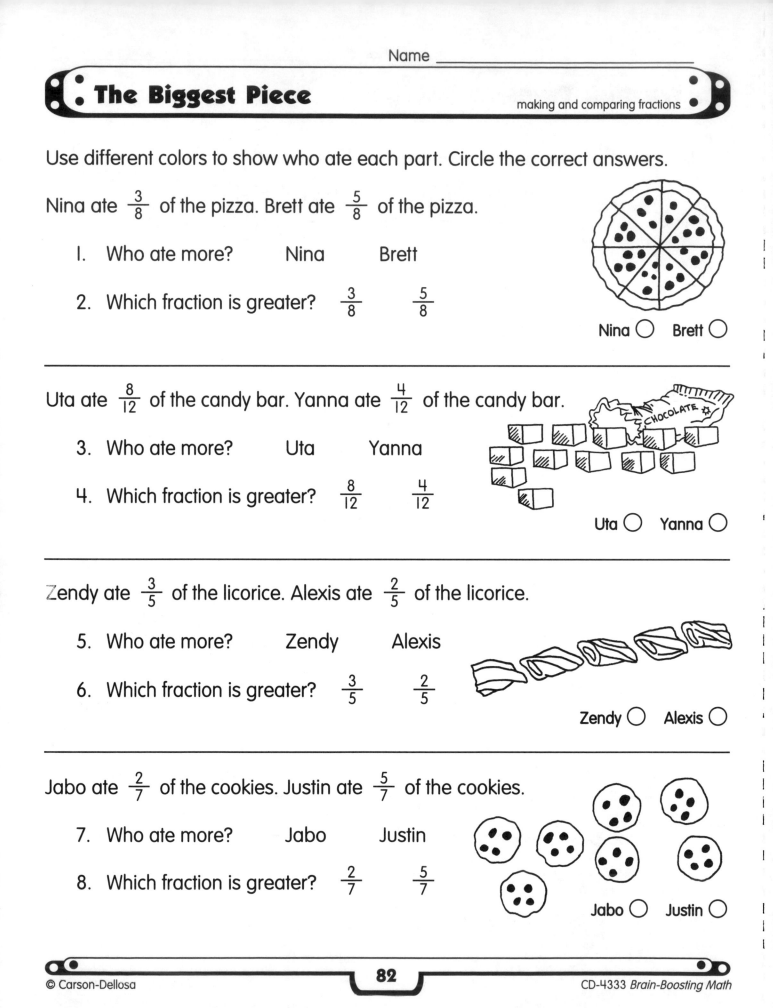

Nina ate $\frac{3}{8}$ of the pizza. Brett ate $\frac{5}{8}$ of the pizza.

1. Who ate more?   Nina   Brett

2. Which fraction is greater? $\frac{3}{8}$ $\frac{5}{8}$

Nina ◯   Brett ◯

Uta ate $\frac{8}{12}$ of the candy bar. Yanna ate $\frac{4}{12}$ of the candy bar.

3. Who ate more?   Uta   Yanna

4. Which fraction is greater? $\frac{8}{12}$ $\frac{4}{12}$

Uta ◯   Yanna ◯

Zendy ate $\frac{3}{5}$ of the licorice. Alexis ate $\frac{2}{5}$ of the licorice.

5. Who ate more?   Zendy   Alexis

6. Which fraction is greater? $\frac{3}{5}$ $\frac{2}{5}$

Zendy ◯   Alexis ◯

Jabo ate $\frac{2}{7}$ of the cookies. Justin ate $\frac{5}{7}$ of the cookies.

7. Who ate more?   Jabo   Justin

8. Which fraction is greater? $\frac{2}{7}$ $\frac{5}{7}$

Jabo ◯   Justin ◯

CD-4333 *Brain-Boosting Math*

The Biggest Piece (continued)

making and comparing fractions

Tyrell ate $\frac{1}{6}$ of the cake.

Brand ate $\frac{3}{6}$ of the cake.

Cobie ate $\frac{2}{6}$ of the cake.

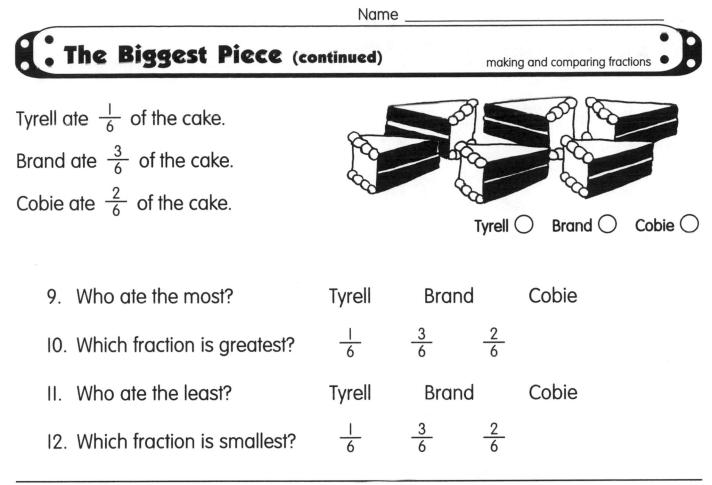

Tyrell ◯   Brand ◯   Cobie ◯

9. Who ate the most?	Tyrell Brand Cobie	
10. Which fraction is greatest?	$\frac{1}{6}$ $\frac{3}{6}$ $\frac{2}{6}$	
11. Who ate the least?	Tyrell Brand Cobie	
12. Which fraction is smallest?	$\frac{1}{6}$ $\frac{3}{6}$ $\frac{2}{6}$	

Riley ate $\frac{3}{10}$ of the grapes.

Ben ate $\frac{2}{10}$ of the grapes.

Jesse ate $\frac{1}{10}$ of the grapes.

Carlos ate $\frac{4}{10}$ of the grapes.

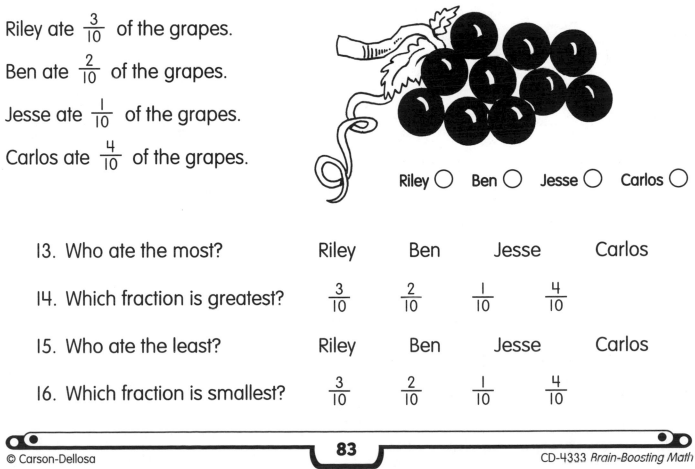

Riley ◯   Ben ◯   Jesse ◯   Carlos ◯

13. Who ate the most?   Riley   Ben   Jesse   Carlos

14. Which fraction is greatest? $\frac{3}{10}$ $\frac{2}{10}$ $\frac{1}{10}$ $\frac{4}{10}$

15. Who ate the least?   Riley   Ben   Jesse   Carlos

16. Which fraction is smallest? $\frac{3}{10}$ $\frac{2}{10}$ $\frac{1}{10}$ $\frac{4}{10}$

CD-4333 *Brain-Boosting Math*

Pop In

Figures that are the same size and shape are called **congruent**.
Figures may be flipped or rotated and still be congruent.

Look at the shapes in the grid. Draw a line from each shape in the grid to a
congruent shape. Color each pair of congruent shapes the same color.

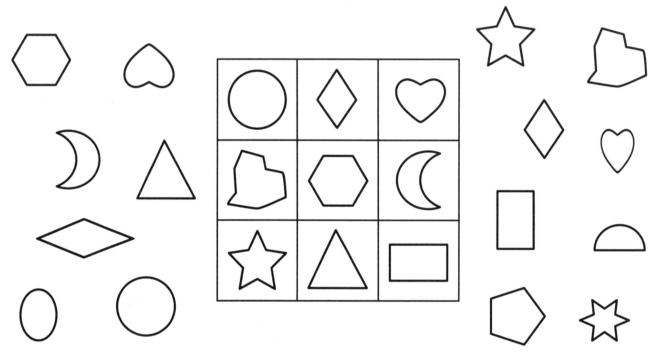

Circle the shape on the right that is congruent to the shape on the left.

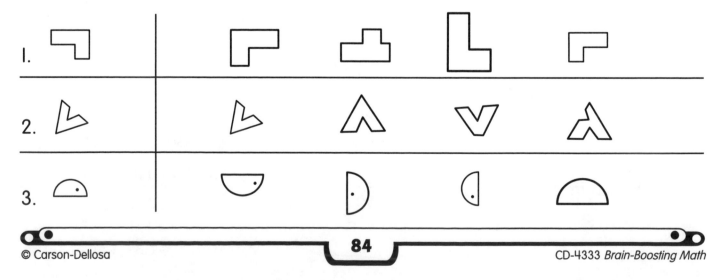

1.

2.

3.

Sea Life

Look at the shapes on the pelicans. Color each shape a different color.

For each pelican, find the fish with a **congruent** shape.
Trace the fish with the same color as the pelican.

For each pelican, find the starfish with a **similar** shape.
Trace each starfish with the same color as the pelican.

Outline each seashell with the same color as a pelican.
Draw a shape on the seashell that is similar to the shape on the pelican.

CD-4333 *Brain-Boosting Math*

Symmetry Search

Look at the picture. Find the objects with at least one line of symmetry.
Draw the line of symmetry.

Tally the number of symmetry lines you found in your search.

Count your tallies. How many? _____

Drawing Symmetry

Draw the line of symmetry in each figure.

1.   2.   3.   4.

Look at the pictures. Half is missing.
Use symmetry to draw the rest of each picture.

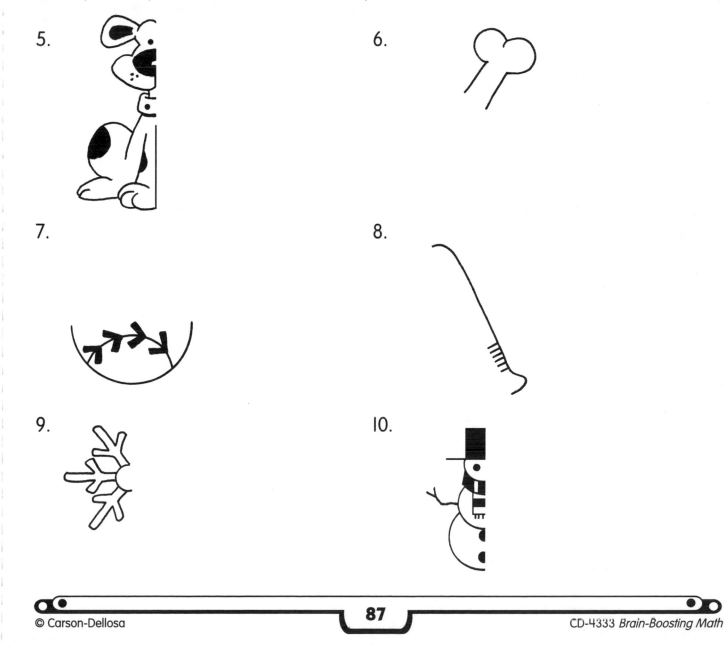

5.

6.

7.

8.

9.

10.

Make the Shape

Review the geometry vocabulary. Then, make the shapes described.

Geometry Vocabulary

polygon ....closed figure with 3 or more sides
triangle ....polygon with 3 sides, 3 vertices
quadrilateral ....polygon with 4 sides, 4 vertices
pentagon ....polygon with 5 sides, 5 vertices
hexagon ....polygon with 6 sides, 6 vertices
octagon ....polygon with 8 sides, 8 vertices
vertex ....point where 2 sides meet
vertices ....more than I vertex

Make each polygon on a geoboard. Record your figure on the grid.
Use a straight edge to make the lines. Count the sides and vertices.
Name the shapes.

1. Make 3 different polygons.

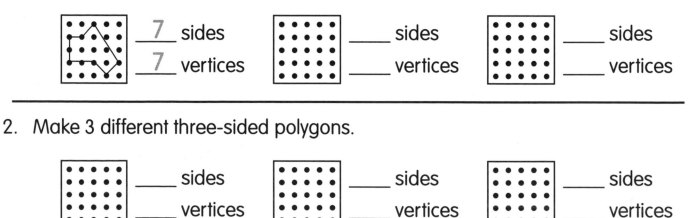

_7_ sides
_7_ vertices

____ sides
____ vertices

____ sides
____ vertices

2. Make 3 different three-sided polygons.

____ sides
____ vertices

____ sides
____ vertices

____ sides
____ vertices

The shapes are all _____.

Make the Shape (continued)

two-dimensional geometry

3. Make 3 different four-sided polygons.

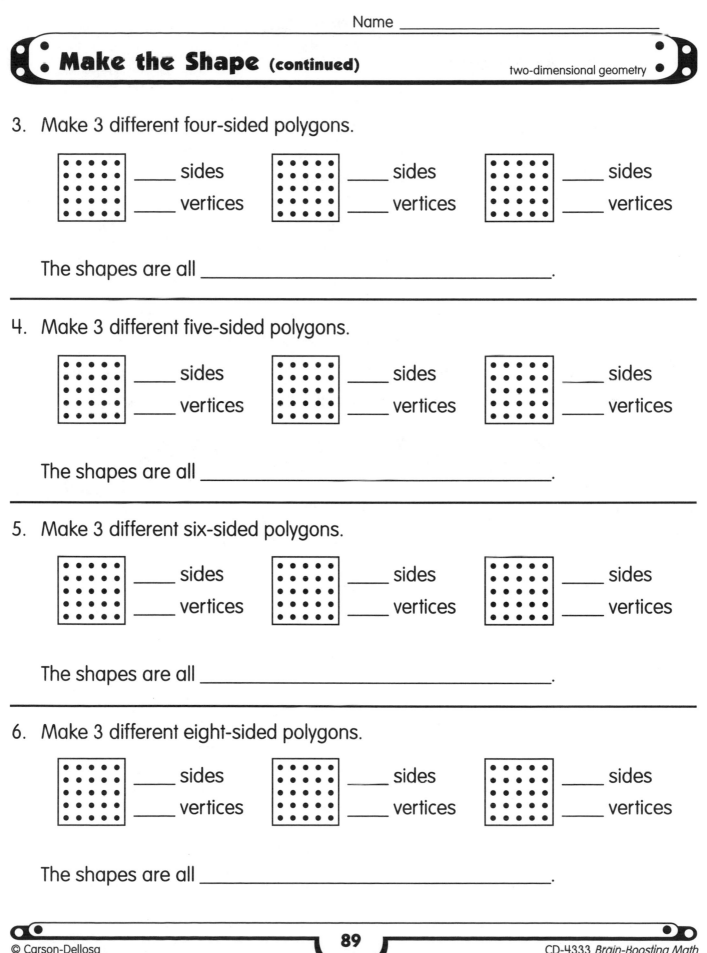

_____ sides

_____ vertices

_____ sides

_____ vertices

_____ sides

_____ vertices

The shapes are all _____.

4. Make 3 different five-sided polygons.

_____ sides

_____ vertices

_____ sides

_____ vertices

_____ sides

_____ vertices

The shapes are all _____.

5. Make 3 different six-sided polygons.

_____ sides

_____ vertices

_____ sides

_____ vertices

_____ sides

_____ vertices

The shapes are all _____.

6. Make 3 different eight-sided polygons.

_____ sides

_____ vertices

_____ sides

_____ vertices

_____ sides

_____ vertices

The shapes are all _____.

CD-4333 *Brain-Boosting Math*

Shape Search

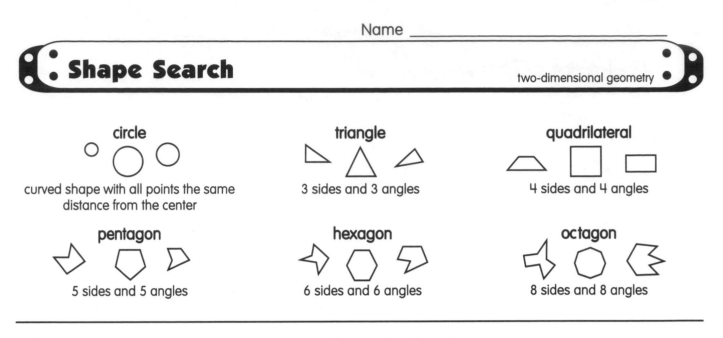

circle

curved shape with all points the same distance from the center

triangle

3 sides and 3 angles

quadrilateral

4 sides and 4 angles

pentagon

5 sides and 5 angles

hexagon

6 sides and 6 angles

octagon

8 sides and 8 angles

Look for the closed figures in the picture. Color the shapes:

circles = red
pentagons = orange

triangles = blue
hexagons = yellow

quadrilaterals = green
octagons = purple

How many? ____ circles   ____ triangles   ____ quadrilaterals

____ pentagons   ____ hexagons   ____ octagons

CD-4333 *Brain-Boosting Math*

Collect the Shapes

two-dimensional geometry/data collection

Look at the shapes on the right. Follow the directions.

1. Color the circles yellow.
2. Color the ovals blue.
3. Color the triangles green.
4. Color the quadrilaterals red.
5. Color the hexagons orange.
6. Color the octagons purple.

7. Use the shapes to make a tally chart. Count each set of tally marks and write the number on the line.

Shape	Number Found
circle	
oval	
triangle	
quadrilateral	
hexagon	
octagon	

_____
_____
_____
_____
_____
_____

8. Color 1 box on the graph for each shape.

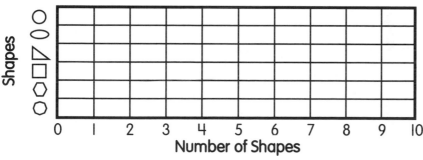

Shapes

Number of Shapes

0 1 2 3 4 5 6 7 8 9 10

9. Write 1 true statement about the graph. Use words like **greater than**, **less than**, **more**, **fewer**, or **equal**.

   CD-4333 *Brain-Boosting Math*

Shape Graph

two-dimensional geometry/understanding graphs

Maria counted all the shapes she found on the pages of her favorite book. She made a graph of the results.

Shapes Found in Maria's Book

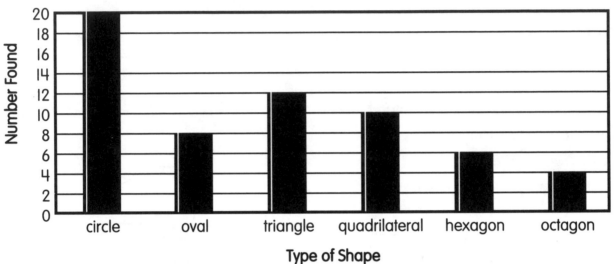

Type of Shape

Use the information from Maria's graph to fill in the frequency table.

Shape	Number Found
circle	
oval	
triangle	
quadrilateral	
hexagon	
octagon	

In the space below, draw all the different shapes Maria found.

3-D Shapes Venn Diagram

Look at the 3-dimensional shapes below. Study the faces, or flat surfaces, of each one. Then, write the number next to each shape in the correct part of the Venn diagram. Don't forget about the outside set!

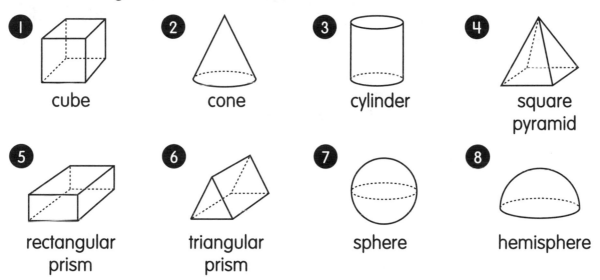

1 cube

2 cone

3 cylinder

4 square pyramid

5 rectangular prism

6 triangular prism

7 sphere

8 hemisphere

Locate objects around the room that fit the categories.
Draw or write the name of each object in the diagram.

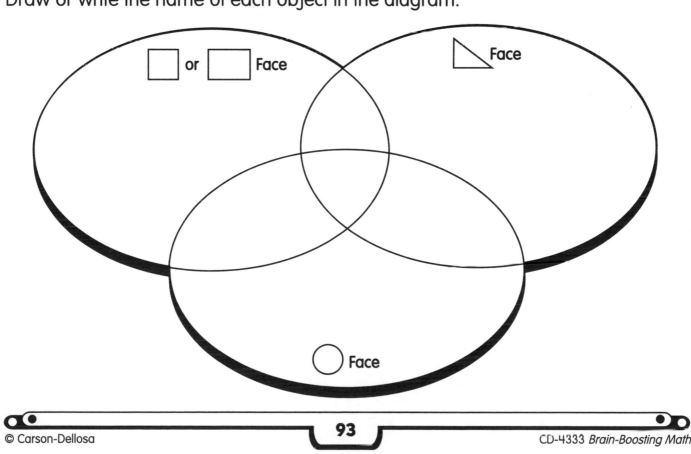

☐ or ☐ Face

△ Face

○ Face

3-D Shapes

Find a model of each shape. Trace over it with your fingers. Write the number of faces, edges, and corners below the picture of each shape.

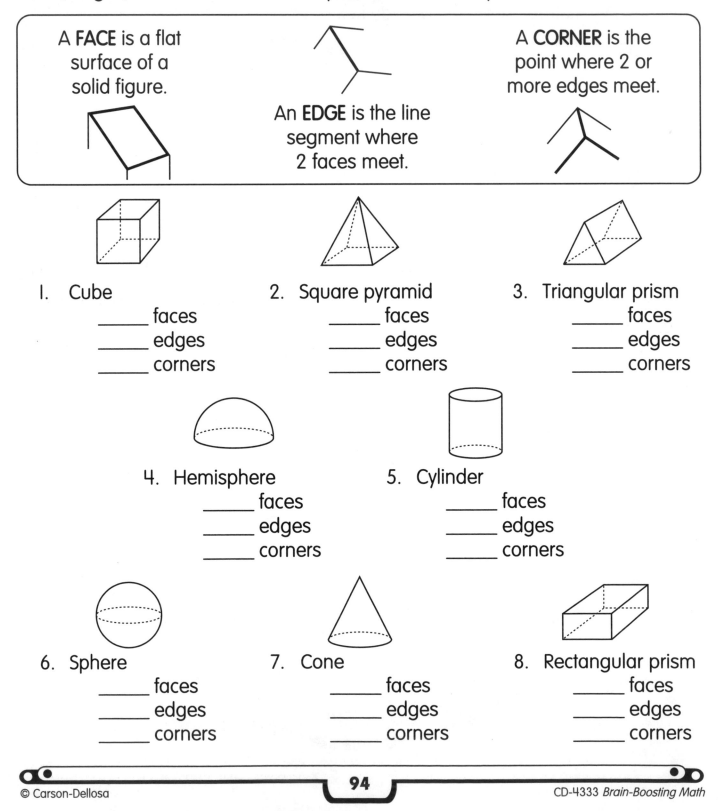

A **FACE** is a flat surface of a solid figure.

An **EDGE** is the line segment where 2 faces meet.

A **CORNER** is the point where 2 or more edges meet.

1. Cube
   _____ faces
   _____ edges
   _____ corners

2. Square pyramid
   _____ faces
   _____ edges
   _____ corners

3. Triangular prism
   _____ faces
   _____ edges
   _____ corners

4. Hemisphere
   _____ faces
   _____ edges
   _____ corners

5. Cylinder
   _____ faces
   _____ edges
   _____ corners

6. Sphere
   _____ faces
   _____ edges
   _____ corners

7. Cone
   _____ faces
   _____ edges
   _____ corners

8. Rectangular prism
   _____ faces
   _____ edges
   _____ corners

CD-4333 *Brain-Boosting Math*

3-D Shapes (continued)

9. Use the information you gathered on page 94 to fill in the table.

Shape	Number of Corners	Number of Edges	Number of Faces
cone			
cube			
cylinder			
hemisphere			
rectangular prism			
sphere			
square pyramid			
triangular prism			

Look again at all 8 shapes.

10. How many have at least 1 ◯ face? _____

    Which shapes? Draw a ◯ next to each shape's name in the table.

11. How many have at least 1 △ face? _____

    Which shapes? Draw a △ next to each shape's name in the table.

12. How many have at least 1 ☐ or ▭ face? _____

    Which shapes? Draw a ☐ next to each shape's name in the table.

CD-4333 *Brain-Boosting Math*

Picnic Blankets

Beula Bear wants to have a picnic for her friends. Help arrange the square blankets so each friend has a place to sit.

◄ Only 1 friend can sit on each side.

Blankets that are next to each other must share 1 full side. ▶   not

Put each set of blankets together in 2 different ways. Draw a picture to show how many friends could sit down at each set of blankets.

1. Use 3 blankets.

2. Use 4 blankets.

3. Use 6 blankets.

4. Use 8 blankets.

5. Beula wants to have 12 spots at her picnic. Show 2 different ways she could put blankets together to fit 12 and only 12 bears.

Mouse House

Help Marvin Mouse choose the best tiles for his mouse house floor.
Look at the size and color of each tile. Draw and color the pattern on the grid.
Each line, start one over in the pattern. Then, answer the questions.

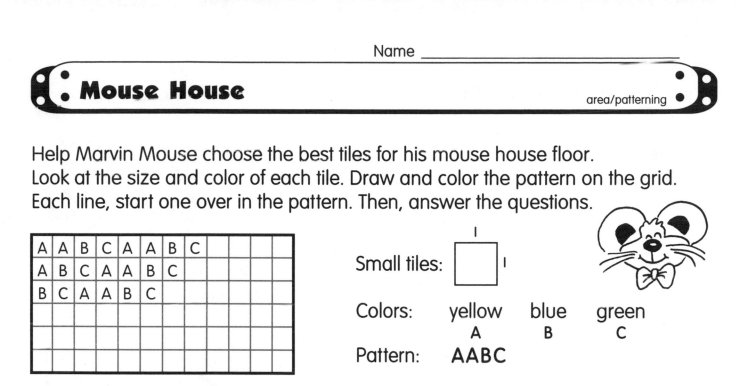

Small tiles:

Colors: yellow blue green
              A   B   C

Pattern: **AABC**

1. How many small tiles are needed to cover the floor? _____

2. If small tiles cost 1¢ each, what would be the total cost? _____

Medium tiles:

Colors: red brown
            A   B

Pattern: **ABBA**

3. How many medium tiles are needed to cover the floor? _____

4. If medium tiles cost 5¢ each, what would be the total cost? _____

Large tiles:

Colors: orange green
              A   B

Pattern: **AB**

5. How many large tiles are needed to cover the floor? _____

6. If large tiles cost 10¢ each, what would be the total cost? _____

7. Which tile would you recommend? Why? Tell a friend.

Capacity Creature

Find the body. It says "I gallon." Color it green.
Find 4 legs. Each leg says "I quart." Color them orange.
Find 8 feet. Each foot says "I pint." Color them purple.
Find 16 toes. Each toe says "I cup." Color them yellow.

Cut out the pieces and put them together to make a Capacity Creature. Look at the picture above to help you. Use the creature to answer the questions on page 99.

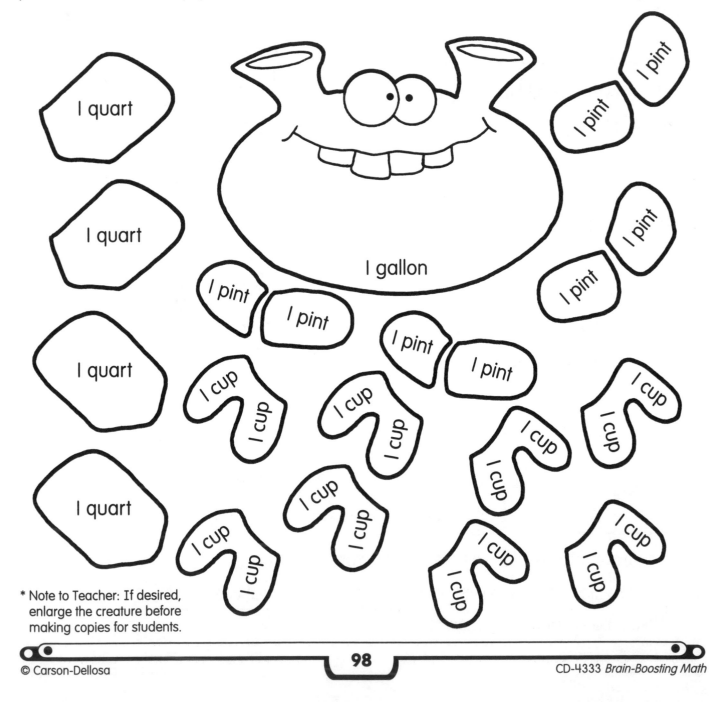

* Note to Teacher: If desired, enlarge the creature before making copies for students.

CD-4333 *Brain-Boosting Math*

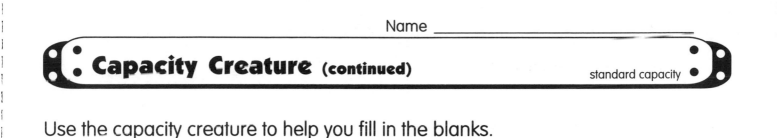
Use the capacity creature to help you fill in the blanks.

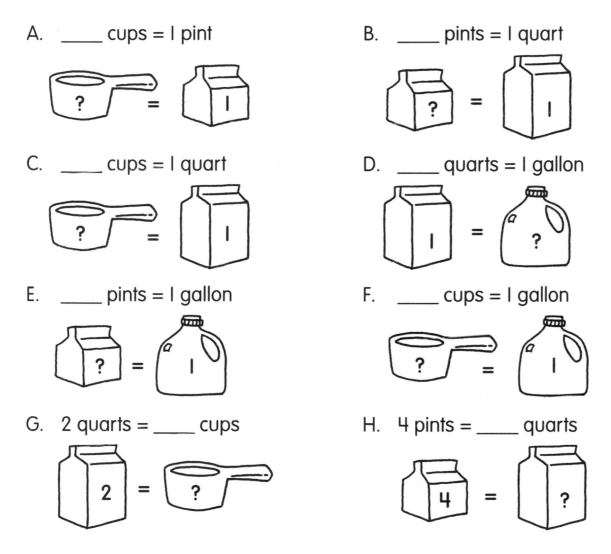

A. _____ cups = 1 pint

B. _____ pints = 1 quart

C. _____ cups = 1 quart

D. _____ quarts = 1 gallon

E. _____ pints = 1 gallon

F. _____ cups = 1 gallon

G. 2 quarts = _____ cups

H. 4 pints = _____ quarts

I. Five friends each want a cup of milk. Is 1 quart enough? _____

Explain. _____

J. Jenn is getting juice for her class. There are 22 students.

Is 1 gallon enough if each student gets 1 cup? _____

Explain. _____

Inching Along

Measure the lines. Write each length in inches.

A. _____ in.

B. _____ in.

C. _____ in.

D. _____ in.

E. _____ in.

Find an object whose length is between A and D. Place one end of the object on the first dot. Draw a second dot at the other end. Measure between the dots to the nearest inch. Record the length and the name of the object.

F. _____ in.   Object: _____

What unit would you use to measure each length? Circle the best choice.

		inches	feet	miles
G.	Length of a pencil	inches	feet	miles
H.	Distance from California to New York	inches	feet	miles
I.	Length of a school hallway	inches	feet	miles
J.	Height of your book	inches	feet	miles
K.	Distance from the earth to the moon	inches	feet	miles
L.	Length of your thumb	inches	feet	miles

Centimeter Search

Measure the lines. Write each length in centimeters.

A. _____ cm

B. _____ cm

C. _____ cm

D. _____ cm

E. _____ cm

F. _____ cm

G. _____ cm

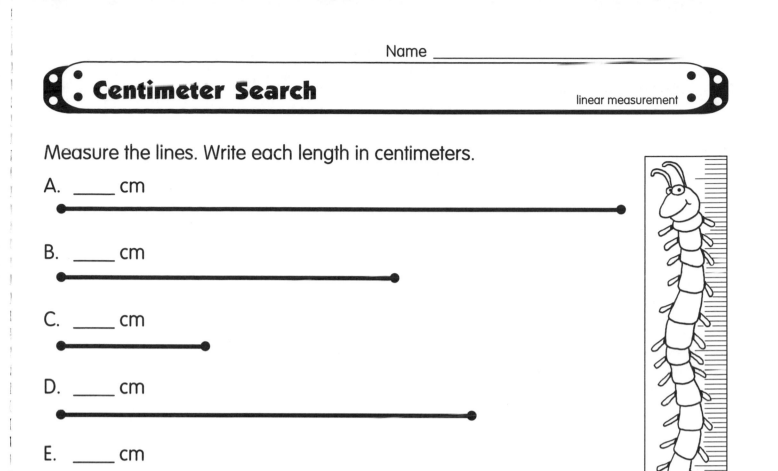

Find objects whose lengths are between the lengths given. Place one end of the object on the first dot. Draw another dot at the other end. Measure between the dots to the nearest centimeter. Record the length and the name of the object.

H. between C and A

_____ cm   Object: _____

I. between E and B

_____ cm   Object: _____

CD-4333 *Brain-Boosting Math*

Pan Balance

Look at the pan balance. Add the values of the mass set. Write the value on the line. Circle **less than**, **equal to**, or **more than**.

1. The mass of the crayon is

    less than
    equal to   _____ grams.
    more than

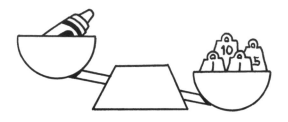

2. The mass of the cup is

    less than
    equal to   _____ grams.
    more than

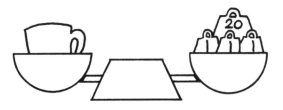

3. The mass of the ruler is

    less than
    equal to   _____ grams.
    more than

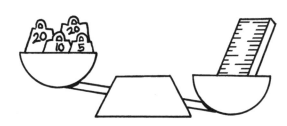

4. The mass of the scissors is

    less than
    equal to   _____ grams.
    more than

5. The mass of the paper clips is

    less than
    equal to   _____ grams.
    more than

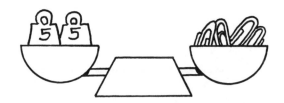

CD-4333 *Brain-Boosting Math*

Money Match

coin values

Count the coins. Write the value. Draw a line to match equal values.

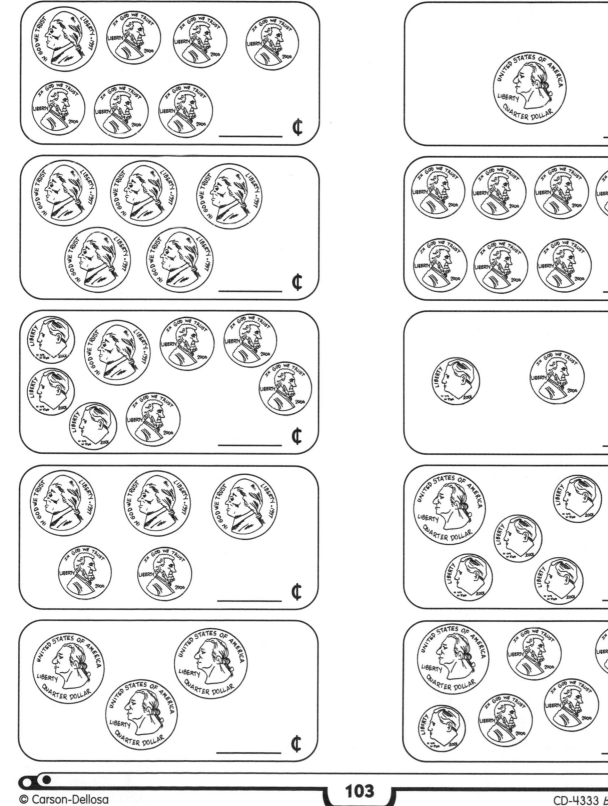

Money Draw

determining value of coin groups

Look at the coins. Write the value. Show another way to make the same amount. You may draw or stamp the coins.

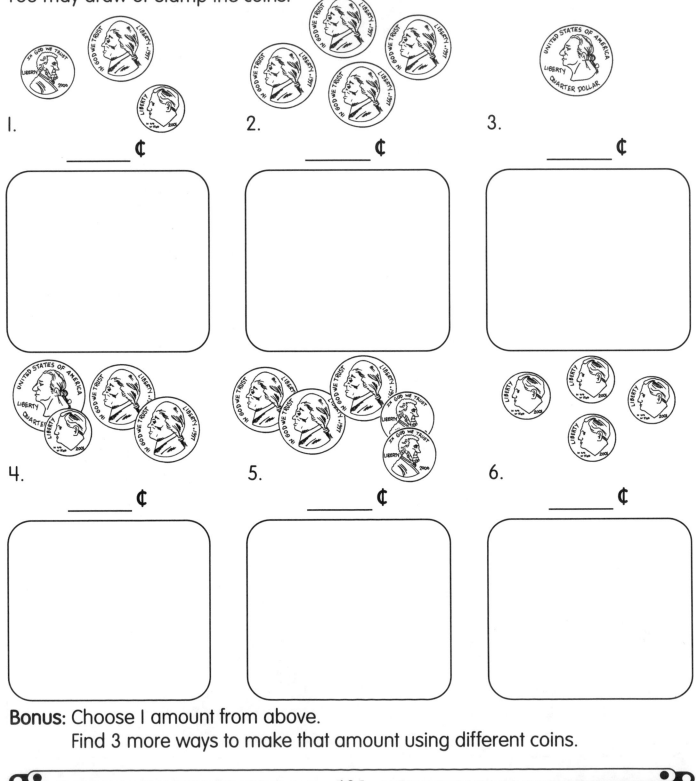

1. _____ ¢

2. _____ ¢

3. _____ ¢

4. _____ ¢

5. _____ ¢

6. _____ ¢

Bonus: Choose 1 amount from above.
Find 3 more ways to make that amount using different coins.

CD-4333 *Brain-Boosting Math*

Who Has More?

Count each group of coins. Write the value.

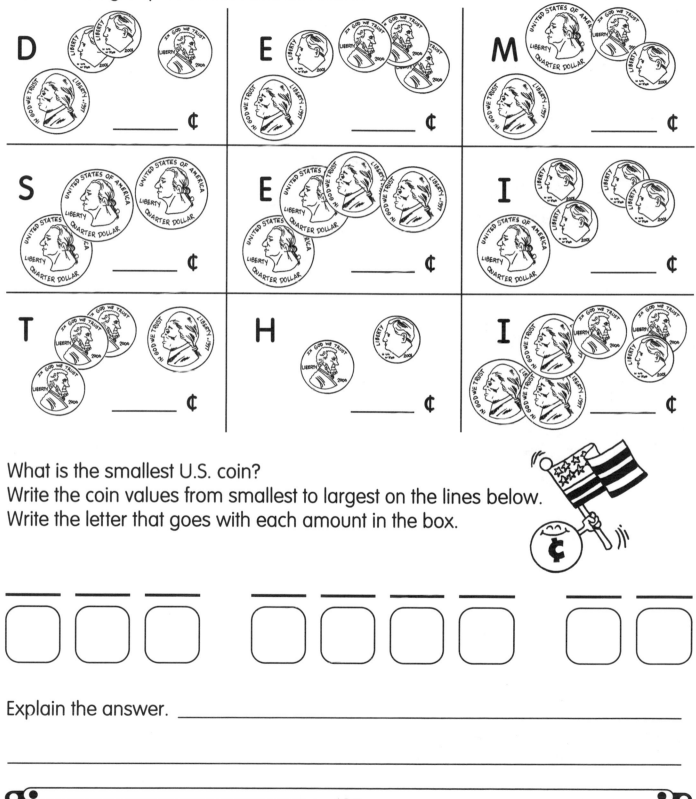

D _____ ¢

E _____ ¢

M _____ ¢

S _____ ¢

E _____ ¢

I _____ ¢

T _____ ¢

H _____ ¢

I _____ ¢

What is the smallest U.S. coin?
Write the coin values from smallest to largest on the lines below.
Write the letter that goes with each amount in the box.

Explain the answer. _____

_____

Money Comparisons

Find the value of each group of coins. Compare the values and write <, >, or = in the circle.

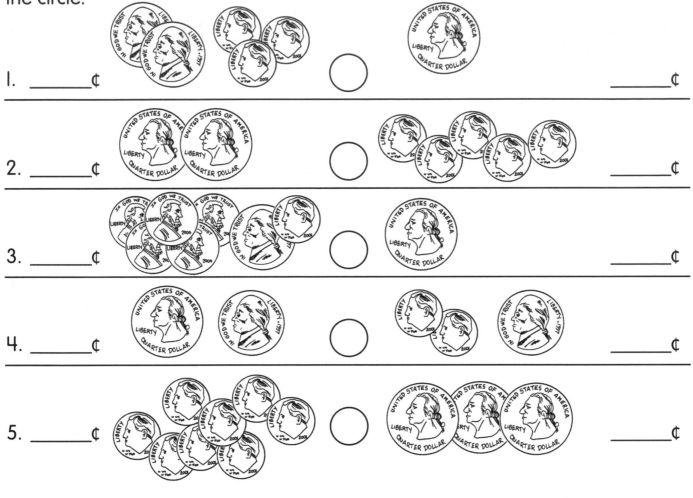

1. _____¢ ⃝ _____¢

2. _____¢ ⃝ _____¢

3. _____¢ ⃝ _____¢

4. _____¢ ⃝ _____¢

5. _____¢ ⃝ _____¢

Draw or stamp your own coin combinations to make each symbol true.

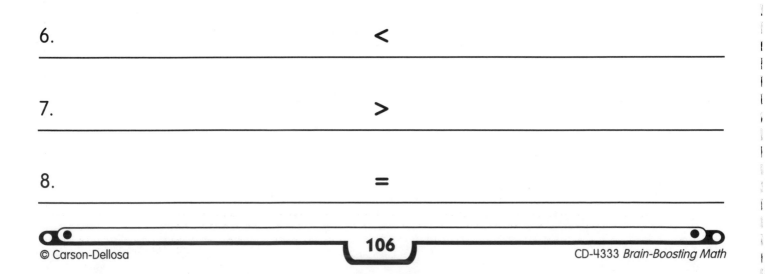

6. _____ < _____

7. _____ > _____

8. _____ = _____

CD-4333 *Brain-Boosting Math*

Which Coins?

money/problem solving

Read. Stamp or draw the coins.
Show more than one way if you can.

Make 40¢.	Make 85¢.	Make 53¢.
1. Taka has 1 quarter. What could the other coins be?	4. Fita has 3 quarters. What could the other coins be?	7. Lara has 6 nickels. What could the other coins be?
2. Kasha has 3 dimes. What could the other coins be?	5. Reba has 4 dimes. What could the other coins be?	8. Rico has 4 dimes. What could the other coins be?
3. Olivia has no dimes or pennies. What could the coins be?	6. Dillon has no nickels or pennies. What could the coins be?	9. Theodore has no dimes. What could the coins be?

CD-4333 *Brain-Boosting Math*

Coin Count

Add or subtract to find the answers.

1. Nell has 9 pennies. She gives 1 to Judy and 3 to Rick.

   How many pennies does she have left? _____

   What is their value? _____

2. Hailey has 12 dimes. She gives 5 to Blake and 3 to Jo. Dan gives her 4 more.

   How many dimes does Hailey have now? _____

   What is their value? _____

3. David has 5 nickels. He finds 6 more.

   How many nickels does David have now? _____

   What is their value? _____

4. Jessie has 16 pennies. She gives Jeni 9 pennies and then finds 2 more.

   How many pennies does she have in all? _____

   What is their value? _____

5. Sydney has 8 nickels. Jordi has 5 nickels.

   How many more nickels does Sydney have? _____

   What is their value? _____

6. Hector has 13 dimes. Meg has 9 dimes.

   How many more dimes does Hector have? _____

   What is their value? _____

Money Graph

Look at the graph. Use the information to complete the tally chart and frequency table. Then, answer the questions.

Coins Saved in Piggy Bank

Coin	Number of Coins
quarter	◯
dime	◯ ◯ ◯
nickel	◯ ◯ ◯
penny	◯ ◯ ◯ ◯ ◯

◯ = 3 coins

1. Make a tally chart.

Coin	Number of Coins
quarter	
dime	
nickel	
penny	

2. Make a frequency table.

Coin	Number of Coins
quarter	
dime	
nickel	
penny	

3. How many quarters are there? _____ What is their total value?_____

4. How many dimes are there? _____ What is their total value?_____

5. How many nickels are there? _____ What is their total value? _____

6. How many pennies are there? _____ What is their total value? _____

7. There are more _____ than any other coins.

8. Which group of coins has the greatest total value? _____

9. There are an equal number of _____ and _____.

10. There are _____ fewer quarters than dimes.

Money Matrix

determining value of coins/mathematical reasoning

Read the clues to find out who has which coins. Use the matrix to help you.

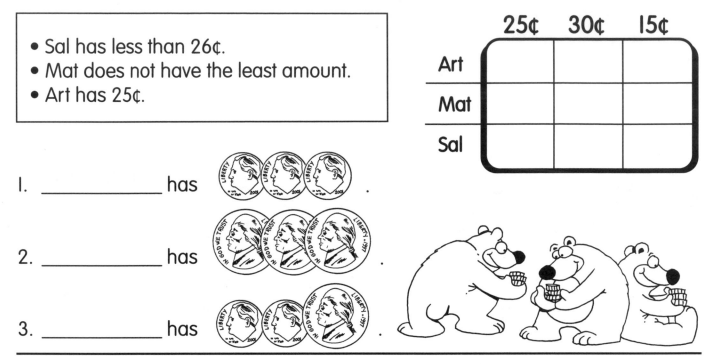

- Sal has less than 26¢.
- Mat does not have the least amount.
- Art has 25¢.

	25¢	30¢	15¢
Art			
Mat			
Sal			

1. _____ has _____ .

2. _____ has _____ .

3. _____ has _____ .

Read the clues to find out who has which coins. Use the matrix to help you.

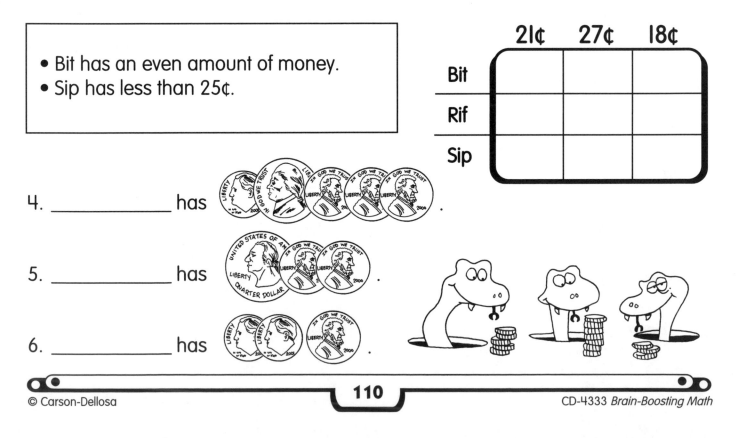

- Bit has an even amount of money.
- Sip has less than 25¢.

	21¢	27¢	18¢
Bit			
Rif			
Sip			

4. _____ has _____ .

5. _____ has _____ .

6. _____ has _____ .

CD-4333 *Brain-Boosting Math*

River Race

Help the animals cross the river. Find and circle each animal's number on the riverbank. Draw a line to join the multiples of the number. You may move down, up, left, right, or diagonally. Use a different color for each animal's path.

one		two		three		four		five			
1	16	2	7	3	15	4	20	5	7	24	16

2	3	4	20	13	6	25	8	25	10	12	30
8	5	6	8	24	30	9	12	30	18	15	26
6	12	10	28	35	20	16	34	15	20	21	35
7	8	14	32	56	40	40	35	33	25	42	24
11	9	18	16	36	44	45	16	30	54	27	49
12	20	10	8	40	17	24	50	18	22	30	25

Use the pathway to write the multiples of each number.

A. 1, ____, ____, ____, ____, ____, ____, ____, ____

B. 2, ____, ____, ____, ____, ____, ____, ____, ____

C. 3, ____, ____, ____, ____, ____, ____, ____, ____

D. 4, ____, ____, ____, ____, ____, ____, ____, ____

E. 5, ____, ____, ____, ____, ____, ____, ____, ____

CD-4333 *Brain-Boosting Math*

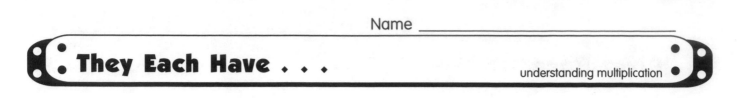

They Each Have . . .

Draw the picture. Write the multiples next to each picture. Use the picture to write an addition sentence. Then, write the multiplication sentence. Label your answer.

Example: Five dogs each have 3 spots. How many spots in all?

3   6   9   12   15

3 + 3 + 3 + 3 + 3 = 15 spots   5 x 3 = 15 spots

1. Two bowls each have 9 apples. How many apples total?

_____   _____

2. Six words each have 3 letters. How many letters in all?

_____   _____

3. Three shirts each have 2 black stripes. How many black stripes in all?

_____   _____

4. Seven envelopes each need 1 stamp. How many stamps are needed?

_____   _____

Write your own description on another piece of paper. Include the word "each."

What If There's More?

Finish each chart. Write multiplication problems for 2 sections of the chart.

1. One pair of scissors has 2 finger holes.

Scissors	1	2	3	4	5	6	7	8	9
Finger holes	2	4	6						

_____
_____

2. One pencil grip has 3 finger marks.

Pencil grip	1	2	3	4	5	6	7	8	9
Finger marks	3	6							

_____
_____

3. One box has 4 pencils in it.

Box	1	2	3	4	5	6	7	8	9
Pencils	4	8							

_____
_____

4. One school week has 5 days.

School week	1	2	3	4	5	6	7	8	9
Days									

_____

Choose information to make your own chart here.

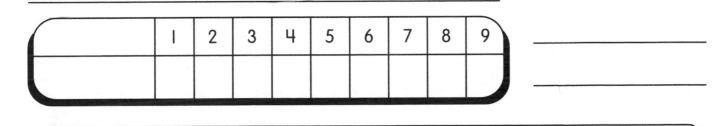

_____

	1	2	3	4	5	6	7	8	9

_____
_____

CD-4333 *Brain-Boosting Math*

Angles and Sides

Use the pictures to answer the questions. If you had the given number of shapes, how many total sides and angles would you have?

A. 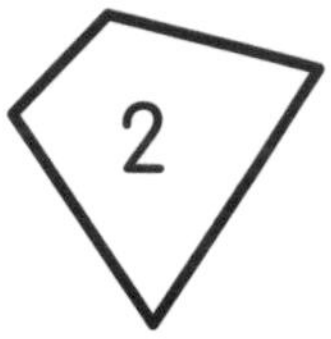 **2**   Total sides? _____

Total angles? _____

B. 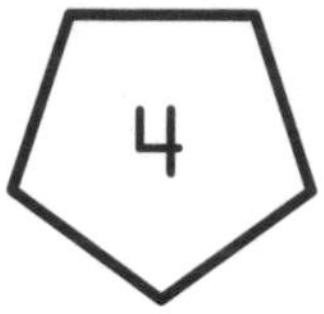 **4**   Total sides? _____

Total angles? _____

C. 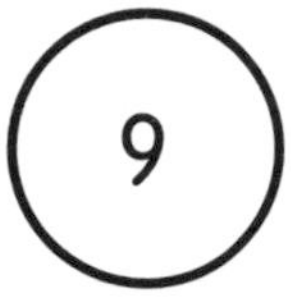 **9**   Total sides? _____

Total angles? _____

D. 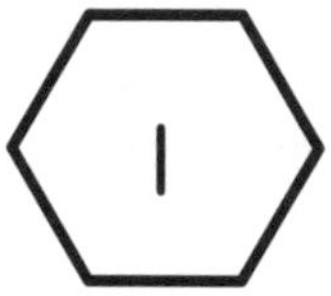 **1**   Total sides? _____

Total angles? _____

E. 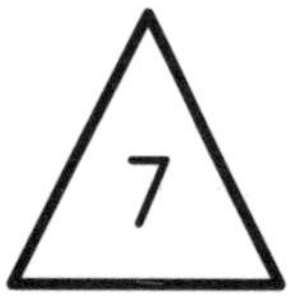 **7**   Total sides? _____

Total angles? _____

F. 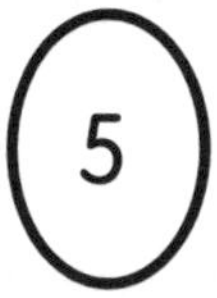 **5**   Total sides? _____

Total angles? _____

G. 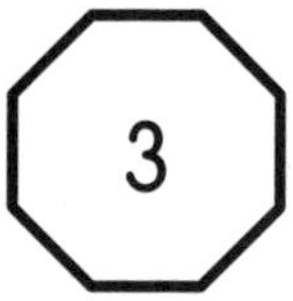 **3**   Total sides? _____

Total angles? _____

H. 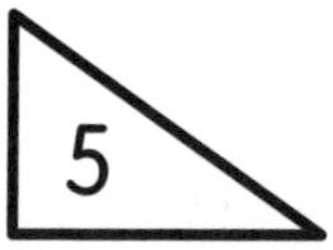 **5**   Total sides? _____

Total angles? _____

I. 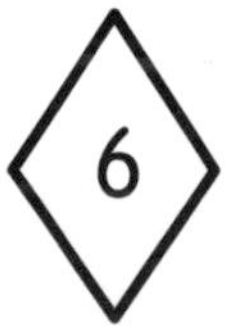 **6**   Total sides? _____

Total angles? _____

J. 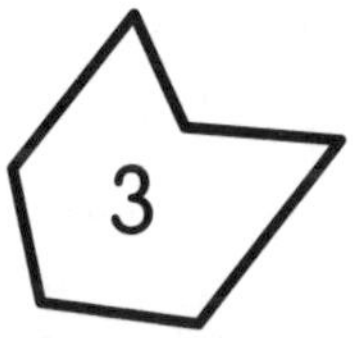 **3**   Total sides? _____

Total angles? _____

Draw the Sets

Draw the sets. Then, write the multiplication problem. Solve.

Example: Five sets of three equals ___15___. ☺☺☺☺☺ $5 \times 3 = 15$

---

1. Four sets of two equals _____.

2. Six sets of one equals _____.

3. Two sets of eight equals _____.

4. Nine sets of two equals _____.

5. One set of nine equals _____.

6. Eight sets of five equals _____.

7. Seven sets of three equals _____.

8. Five sets of four equals _____.

9. Two sets of seven equals _____.

10. Six sets of four equals _____.

11. Four sets of three equals _____.

12. Three sets of six equals _____.

CD-4333 *Brain-Boosting Math*

Filling Sets

Gather objects to make sets. Make the sets shown and fill in the chart.
Choose your own sets to complete the last 5 rows of the chart.

Number of Sets	Number in Each Set	Total Number or Product	Multiplication Sentence
3	2	6	3 x 2 = 6
2	4		
6	2		
4	3		
5	1		

Choose 4 multiplication sentences from the chart.
Write the multiplication sentence and draw the sets for each here.

I.	2.
3.	4.

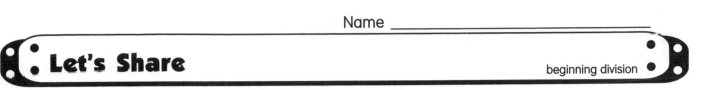

Let's Share

Circle to show a fair share. Write how many each person gets.
Are there any left over? Write **yes** or **no**.

1.

Share with 3.

Each gets _____.   Any left? _____

2.

Share with 6.

Each gets _____.   Any left? _____

3.

Share with 8.

Each gets _____.   Any left? _____

4.

Share with 2.

Each gets _____.   Any left? _____

5.

Share with 2.

Each gets _____.   Any left? _____

6.

Share with 3.

Each gets _____.   Any left? _____

7.

Share with 2.

Each gets _____.   Any left? _____

8.

Share with 5.

Each gets _____.   Any left? _____

Draw and write your own.

Share with _____.

Each gets _____.   Any left? _____

Fishbowl

Draw the items in the fishbowls. Put the same number in each bowl.

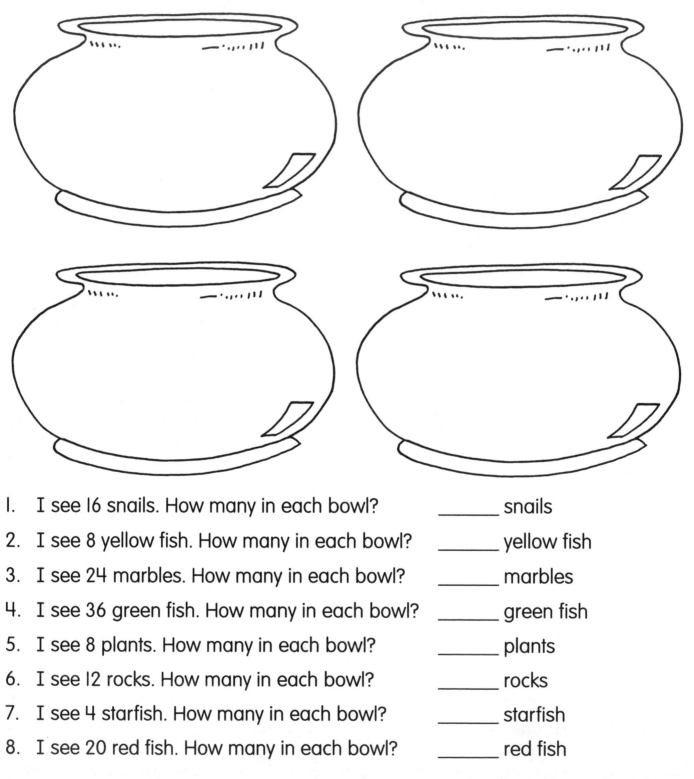

1. I see 16 snails. How many in each bowl?   _____ snails

2. I see 8 yellow fish. How many in each bowl?   _____ yellow fish

3. I see 24 marbles. How many in each bowl?   _____ marbles

4. I see 36 green fish. How many in each bowl?   _____ green fish

5. I see 8 plants. How many in each bowl?   _____ plants

6. I see 12 rocks. How many in each bowl?   _____ rocks

7. I see 4 starfish. How many in each bowl?   _____ starfish

8. I see 20 red fish. How many in each bowl?   _____ red fish

CD-4333 *Brain-Boosting Math*

Picnic at the Beach

Make a picture about a beach picnic. Include the sets described below. Draw the sets in the picture frame. Then, write the answer on the line.

1. Draw a total of 6 shovels in equal groups in 3 pails.

[ ] shovels each

2. Draw a total of 9 windows in equal groups on 3 sand castles.

[ ] windows each

3. Draw a total of 10 ants in equal groups on 2 sandwiches.

[ ] ants each

4. Draw a total of 12 seeds in equal groups on 3 pieces of watermelon.

[ ] seeds each

Write your own.

5. I drew a total of _____ _____

   in equal groups on _____ _____.

[ ]

_____ each

Organization

Read carefully. Draw the sets.

1. Gita has 24 pencils. She wants to put them in bags. Each bag must have the same number of pencils. Show two ways to put the pencils in bags.

2. Jade has 20 seashells. She wants to store them in boxes. Each box must have the same number of shells. Show two ways to store the shells in boxes.

3. Ulio has 12 trophies. He wants to put them on shelves. Each shelf needs the same number of trophies. Show two ways to put the trophies on shelves.

4. Ian has 28 grapes. He wants to put them in cups. Each cup needs the same number of grapes. Show two ways to put the grapes in cups.

5. Suki has 16 cupcakes. She wants to put them on plates. Each plate needs the same number of cupcakes. Show two ways to put the cupcakes on plates.

6. Meg has 18 drawings. She wants to hang them in equal groups on her walls. Show two ways to hang the drawings on the walls.

p. 5 — Draw This
Pictures will vary but should follow the directions given.

p. 10 — Color Correctly
Colors from left to right should be:
1. red, blue, green, yellow, orange, purple, black, brown, white, pink
2. blue, pink, red, black, white, green, yellow, orange, purple, brown

p. 12 — Patterning
1. AB   2. ABBC   3. ABCD   4. AABBC
5. ABBBC
Student examples will vary but should follow the patterns described.

p. 13 — Pattern Practice
1–6. Examples will vary but should follow the patterns described.
7. sun, sun
8. square, triangle

p. 14 — Pattern Problems
1. ant   2. ladybug
3. star, moon, moon, star, moon, moon
4. moon   5. seven   6. dog
7. mouse, dog, cat, mouse, dog, mouse, dog, cat, mouse, dog

p. 15 — It's in the Order
1. hat, mitten, shoe
2. cat, dog, mouse
3. bus, truck, car
4. baseball, football, soccer ball

p. 16 — Number Patterns
A. 49, 50, 51, 52; ||||| ••
B. 72, 71, 70, 69; ||||||•••••••••
C. 44, 46, 48, 50; |||||
D. 85, 90, 95, 100; ❑
E. 380, 390, 400, 410; ❑❑❑❑|
F. 500, 600, 700, 800; ❑❑❑❑❑❑❑❑
G. 830, 825, 820, 815;
   ❑❑❑❑❑❑❑❑|•••••
H. 725, 715, 705, 695;
   ❑❑❑❑❑❑|||||||||•••••

p. 17 — Leapfrog
A. 6, 18, 25, 44
B. 52, 65, 96, 100
C. 103, 179, 281, 405
D. 537, 601, 670, 768
E. 220, 347, 374, 383
Numbers added by the student will vary but should fall between the two numbers around them.

p. 18 — Quackers
All possible combinations are listed in descending order. Answers must include the first and last numbers, but the middle numbers may vary.
A. 872, 827, 782, 728, 287, 278
B. 931, 913, 391, 319, 193, 139
C. 964, 946, 694, 649, 496, 469
D. 7521, 7512, 7251, 7215, 7152, 7125, 5721, 5712, 5271, 5217, 5172, 5127, 2751, 2715, 2571, 2517, 2175, 2157, 1752, 1725, 1572, 1527, 1275, 1257
E. 8643, 8634, 8463, 8436, 8364, 8346, 6843, 6834, 6483, 6438, 6384, 6348, 4863, 4836, 4683, 4638, 4386, 4368, 3864, 3846, 3684, 3648, 3486, 3468
F. Answers will vary.

p. 19 — Higher or Lower?
A. 75; between 50 and 75
B. 65; between 50 and 65
C. 56; between 56 and 65
D. 60; between 60 and 65
E. 63; between 60 and 63
F. 61; between 61 and 63; The number is 62.
Game 2
A. 60; between 20 and 60
B. 35; between 20 and 35
C. 26; between 26 and 35
D. 29; between 26 and 29
E. 28; between 26 and 28; The number is 27.

pp. 20–21 — Numbers in the Box
1. a. 820; b. 443; c. 578; d. 578
2. a. 341; b. 578; c. 443; d. 820
3. a. 578, 820; b. 341, 259, 97, 443
4. a. 97, 259, 341, 443, 578, 820
   b. 820, 578, 443, 341, 259, 97
5. a. 578 = ❑❑❑❑❑|||||||••••••••
   b. 321 = ❑❑❑||•
   c. 259 = ❑❑|||||•••••••••
   d. 97 = |||||||||••••••••
   e. 820 = ❑❑❑❑❑❑❑❑ ||
   f. 443 = ❑❑❑❑|||| •••
6. Answers will vary.

p. 22 — Put It Away
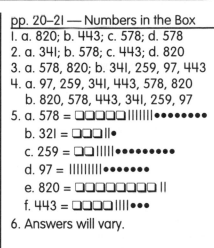

p. 23 — Bagglers' Bins
A. (1, 4)   B. (1, 2)   C. (3, 2)
D. (4, 3)   E. (5, 4)   F. (2, 1)

pp. 24–25 — Is It Certain?
1. impossible   2. maybe
3. impossible   4. certain
5. maybe   6. maybe
7. impossible   8. impossible
9. maybe   10. certain
11. maybe   12. maybe
13. impossible   14. impossible
15. certain   16. impossible
17. maybe   18. maybe
19. maybe   20. certain

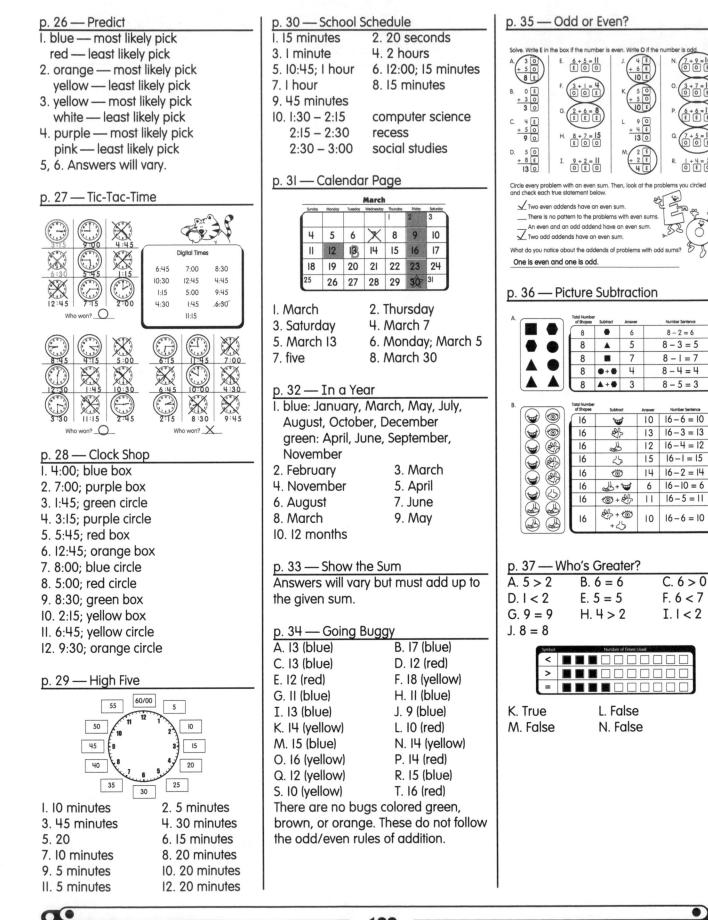

p. 26 — Predict

1. blue — most likely pick
   red — least likely pick
2. orange — most likely pick
   yellow — least likely pick
3. yellow — most likely pick
   white — least likely pick
4. purple — most likely pick
   pink — least likely pick
5, 6. Answers will vary.

p. 27 — Tic-Tac-Time

Who won? ○

Who won? ○   Who won? X

p. 28 — Clock Shop

1. 4:00; blue box
2. 7:00; purple box
3. 1:45; green circle
4. 3:15; purple circle
5. 5:45; red box
6. 12:45; orange box
7. 8:00; blue circle
8. 5:00; red circle
9. 8:30; green box
10. 2:15; yellow box
11. 6:45; yellow circle
12. 9:30; orange circle

p. 29 — High Five

1. 10 minutes   2. 5 minutes
3. 45 minutes   4. 30 minutes
5. 20   6. 15 minutes
7. 10 minutes   8. 20 minutes
9. 5 minutes   10. 20 minutes
11. 5 minutes   12. 20 minutes

p. 30 — School Schedule

1. 15 minutes   2. 20 seconds
3. 1 minute   4. 2 hours
5. 10:45; 1 hour   6. 12:00; 15 minutes
7. 1 hour   8. 15 minutes
9. 45 minutes
10. 1:30 – 2:15   computer science
    2:15 – 2:30   recess
    2:30 – 3:00   social studies

p. 31 — Calendar Page

1. March   2. Thursday
3. Saturday   4. March 7
5. March 13   6. Monday; March 5
7. five   8. March 30

p. 32 — In a Year

1. blue: January, March, May, July,
   August, October, December
   green: April, June, September,
   November
2. February   3. March
4. November   5. April
6. August   7. June
8. March   9. May
10. 12 months

p. 33 — Show the Sum

Answers will vary but must add up to
the given sum.

p. 34 — Going Buggy

A. 13 (blue)   B. 17 (blue)
C. 13 (blue)   D. 12 (red)
E. 12 (red)   F. 18 (yellow)
G. 11 (blue)   H. 11 (blue)
I. 13 (blue)   J. 9 (blue)
K. 14 (yellow)   L. 10 (red)
M. 15 (blue)   N. 14 (yellow)
O. 16 (yellow)   P. 14 (red)
Q. 12 (yellow)   R. 15 (blue)
S. 10 (yellow)   T. 16 (red)
There are no bugs colored green,
brown, or orange. These do not follow
the odd/even rules of addition.

p. 35 — Odd or Even?

Solve. Write E in the box if the number is even. Write O if the number is odd.

Circle every problem with an even sum. Then, look at the problems you circled and check each true statement below.

✓ Two even addends have an even sum.
___ There is no pattern to the problems with even sums.
___ An even and an odd addend have an even sum.
✓ Two odd addends have an even sum.

What do you notice about the addends of problems with odd sums?
One is even and one is odd.

p. 36 — Picture Subtraction

A.

Total Number of Shapes	Subtract	Answer	Number Sentence
8	●	6	8 – 2 = 6
8	▲	5	8 – 3 = 5
8	■	7	8 – 1 = 7
8	● + ●	4	8 – 4 = 4
8	▲ + ●	3	8 – 5 = 3

B.

Total Number of Shapes	Subtract	Answer	Number Sentence
16		10	16 – 6 = 10
16		13	16 – 3 = 13
16		12	16 – 4 = 12
16		15	16 – 1 = 15
16		14	16 – 2 = 14
16		6	16 – 10 = 6
16		11	16 – 5 = 11
16		10	16 – 6 = 10

p. 37 — Who's Greater?

A. 5 > 2   B. 6 = 6   C. 6 > 0
D. 1 < 2   E. 5 = 5   F. 6 < 7
G. 9 = 9   H. 4 > 2   I. 1 < 2
J. 8 = 8

Symbol	Number of Times Used
<	■ ■ ■ □ □ □ □ □ □ □ □ □
>	■ ■ ■ □ □ □ □ □ □ □ □ □
=	■ ■ ■ ■ □ □ □ □ □ □ □ □

K. True   L. False
M. False   N. False

CD-4333 *Brain-Boosting Math*

p. 38 — Color by Number

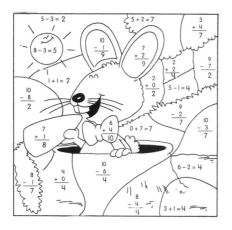

p. 40 — Spiders

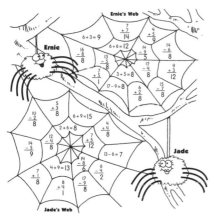

Ernie wins the game.

p. 41 — Bead It

A. 1 + 4 = 5, 4 + 1 = 5, 5 – 1 = 4,
   5 – 4 = 1

B. 5 + 3 = 8, 3 + 5 = 8, 8 – 5 = 3,
   8 – 3 = 5

C. 4 + 2 = 6, 2 + 4 = 6, 6 – 4 = 2,
   6 – 2 = 4

D. 6 + 3 = 9, 3 + 6 = 9, 9 – 6 = 3,
   9 – 3 = 6

E. 3 + 4 = 7, 4 + 3 = 7, 7 – 3 = 4,
   7 – 4 = 3

F. 6 + 4 = 10, 4 + 6 = 10, 10 – 6 = 4,
   10 – 4 = 6

p. 42 — Addition Table

+	0	1	2	3	4	5	6	7	8	9	10
0	0	1	2	3	4	5	6	7	8	9	10
1	1	2	3	4	5	6	7	8	9	10	11
2	2	3	4	5	6	7	8	9	10	11	12
3	3	4	5	6	7	8	9	10	11	12	13
4	4	5	6	7	8	9	10	11	12	13	14
5	5	6	7	8	9	10	11	12	13	14	15
6	6	7	8	9	10	11	12	13	14	15	16
7	7	8	9	10	11	12	13	14	15	16	17
8	8	9	10	11	12	13	14	15	16	17	18
9	9	10	11	12	13	14	15	16	17	18	19
10	10	11	12	13	14	15	16	17	18	19	20

A. 5 + 5, 7 + 3, 17 – 7

B. 2 + 5, 11 – 4, 3 + 4

C. 8 – 4, 2 + 2, 5 – 1

D. 15 – 6, 2 + 7, 11 – 2

E. 11 – 9, 9 – 7, 1 + 1

F. 15 – 10, 2 + 3, 8 – 3

G. Answers will vary.

p. 43 — Pathway

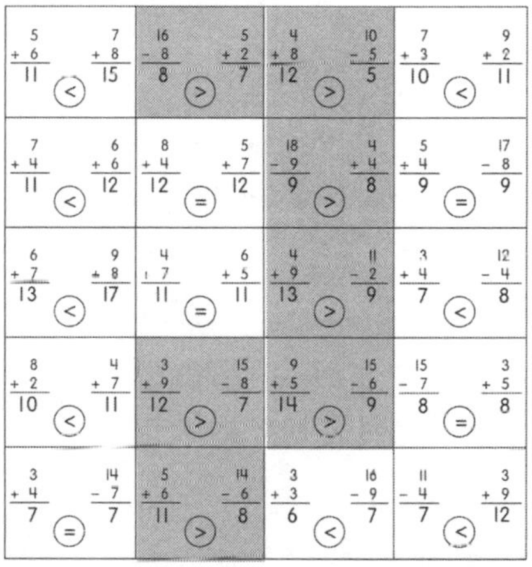

5 + 6 = 11 (<)	16 + 8 = 15	5 – 8 = 8 (>)	5 + 2 = 7 (12) (>)	4 + 8 = 12	10 – 5 = 5 (<)	7 + 3 = 10 (<)	2 + 9 = 11
7 + 4 = 11 (<)	6 + 6 = 12	8 + 4 = 12 (=)	5 + 7 = 12	18 – 9 = 9 (>)	4 + 4 = 8 (>)	5 + 4 = 9	17 – 8 = 9 (=)
6 + 7 = 13 (<)	9 + 8 = 17	4 + 7 = 11 (=)	6 + 5 = 11	4 + 9 = 13 (>)	11 – 2 = 9	3 + 4 = 4	12 – 4 = 8 (<)
8 + 2 = 10 (<)	4 + 7 = 11	3 + 9 = 12 (>)	15 – 8 = 7	9 + 5 = 14 (>)	15 – 6 = 9	15 – 7 = 7	3 + 5 = 8 (=)
3 + 4 = 7 (=)	14 – 7 = 7	5 + 6 = 11 (>)	14 – 6 = 8	3 + 3 = 6 (<)	16 – 9 = 7	11 – 4 = 7	3 + 9 = 12

p. 44 — Tic-Tac-Toe

<!-- tic-tac-toe grids -->

Make a tally chart to show who won the most games.

even	IIII
odd	III
no one	I

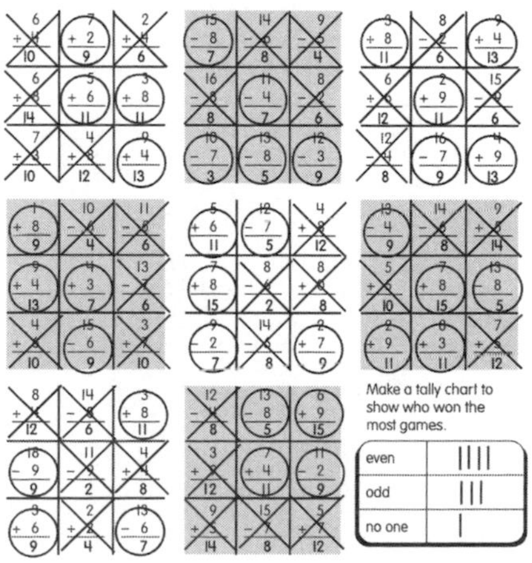

p. 45 — Chain of Equalities

The following number sentences or numbers do not belong:

A. 14 + 3	B. 3 + 8
C. 4 + 6	D. 2 + 9
E. 8	F. 7 + 1
G. 5 + 2	H. 11 – 3

Student number sentences will vary.

p. 46 — Operation

A. +	B. –	C. +	D. +
E. –	F. –	G. +	H. –
I. +	J. +	K. –	L. +
M. –	N. +	O. +	P. –
Q. +	R. +	S. –	T. +
U. +	V. –	W. +	X. –

Symbol	Number of Times
+	IIII IIII IIII IIII
–	IIII IIII

Symbol	Number of Times
+	14
–	10

p. 47 — Same Answer

A. 6	B. 11	C. 13	D. 16
E. 1	F. 4	G. 3	H. 14
I. 9	J. 15	K. 10	L. 18
M. 12	N. 10	O. 17	

Additional number sentences will vary.

pp. 48–49 — Homework Machine

A. 13, 25, 47, 96, 15, 29, 34, 65

B. 11, 5, 18, 46, 62, 7, 29, 38

C. 24, 3, 10, 36, 60, 33, 85, 18

D. 38, 6, 61, 27, 9, 15, 54, 89

E. 39, 23, 64, 12, 6, 55, 91, 67

F. rule: + 5; 68, 50, 24, 11, 18

G. rule: x 2 (double); 4, 40, 12, 6, 62

H. rule: – 3; 21, 62, 93, 4, 9

I. rule: + 20; 55, 92, 30, 61, 24

J. rule: – 2; 34, 25, 62, 83, 47

p. 50 — Make That Number

Answers will vary.

p. 51 — Letter Math

1. 1 + 4 + 4 = 9

2. 3 + 1 + 5 + 3 = 12

3. 4 + 2 + 1 + 1 + 3 + 5 = 16

4. 5 + 2 + 1 + 1 + 2 = 11

5. 3 + 5 + 4 + 4 + 4 = 20

6. 2 + 3 + 1 + 1 + 3 = 10

7. 12 + 8 + 6 = 26

8–11. Answers will vary.

CD-4333 *Brain-Boosting Math*

p. 52 — What Number Am I?
1. two   2. eight
3. five   4. thirteen
5. seven   6. six
7. four   8. four
9. eight   10. eleven
11. one   12. fourteen

p. 53 — What Is Missing?
A. 5   B. 3   C. 11   D. 9
E. 5   F. 1   G. 4   H. 3
I. 7   J. 11   K. 5   L. 8

p. 54 — Hidden Pathways
Other solutions may be possible.

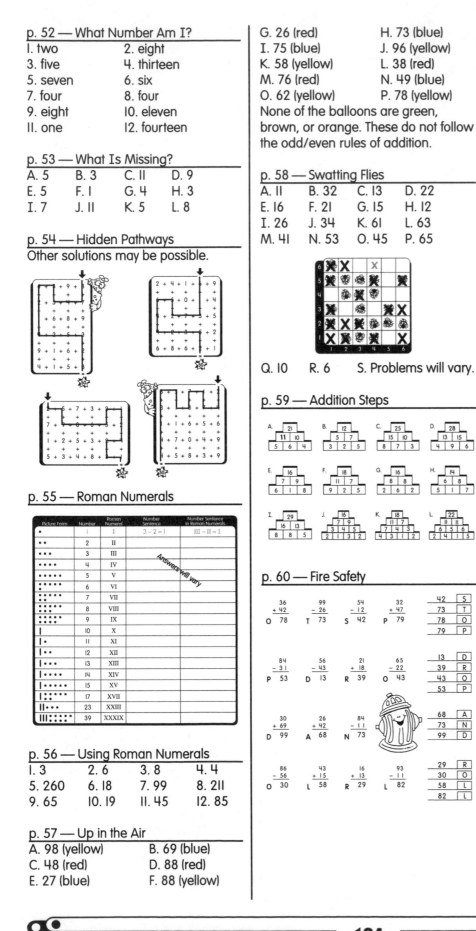

p. 55 — Roman Numerals

Picture Form	Number	Roman Numeral	Number Sentence	Number Sentence in Roman Numerals
•	1	I	3 − 2 = 1	III − II = I
••	2	II		
•••	3	III		
••••	4	IV	Answers will vary	
•••••	5	V		
••••••	6	VI		
•••••••	7	VII		
••••••••	8	VIII		
•••••••••	9	IX		
I	10	X		
I •	11	XI		
I ••	12	XII		
I •••	13	XIII		
I ••••	14	XIV		
I •••••	15	XV		
I •••••••	17	XVII		
II •••	23	XXIII		
III •••••••	39	XXXIX		

p. 56 — Using Roman Numerals
1. 3   2. 6   3. 8   4. 4
5. 260   6. 18   7. 99   8. 211
9. 65   10. 19   11. 45   12. 85

p. 57 — Up in the Air
A. 98 (yellow)   B. 69 (blue)
C. 48 (red)   D. 88 (red)
E. 27 (blue)   F. 88 (yellow)

(continued)
G. 26 (red)   H. 73 (blue)
I. 75 (blue)   J. 96 (yellow)
K. 58 (yellow)   L. 38 (red)
M. 76 (red)   N. 49 (blue)
O. 62 (yellow)   P. 78 (yellow)
None of the balloons are green, brown, or orange. These do not follow the odd/even rules of addition.

p. 58 — Swatting Flies
A. 11   B. 32   C. 13   D. 22
E. 16   F. 21   G. 15   H. 12
I. 26   J. 34   K. 61   L. 63
M. 41   N. 53   O. 45   P. 65

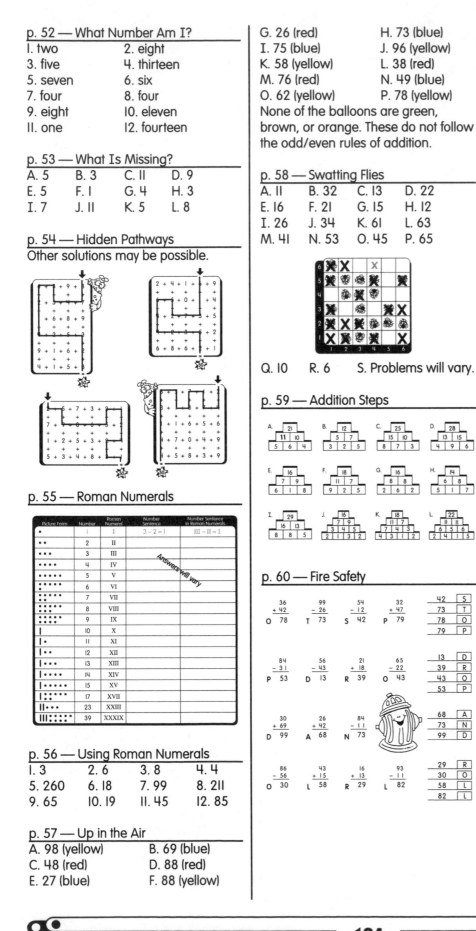

Q. 10   R. 6   S. Problems will vary.

p. 59 — Addition Steps

p. 60 — Fire Safety

p. 61 — Dot-to-Dot

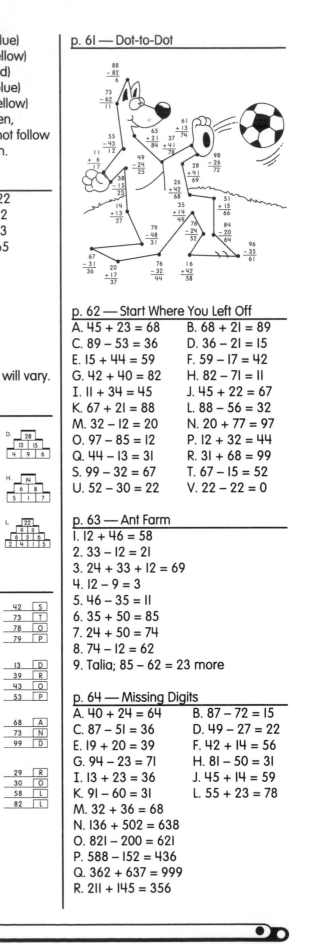

p. 62 — Start Where You Left Off
A. 45 + 23 = 68   B. 68 + 21 = 89
C. 89 − 53 = 36   D. 36 − 21 = 15
E. 15 + 44 = 59   F. 59 − 17 = 42
G. 42 + 40 = 82   H. 82 − 71 = 11
I. 11 + 34 = 45   J. 45 + 22 = 67
K. 67 + 21 = 88   L. 88 − 56 = 32
M. 32 − 12 = 20   N. 20 + 77 = 97
O. 97 − 85 = 12   P. 12 + 32 = 44
Q. 44 − 13 = 31   R. 31 + 68 = 99
S. 99 − 32 = 67   T. 67 − 15 = 52
U. 52 − 30 = 22   V. 22 − 22 = 0

p. 63 — Ant Farm
1. 12 + 46 = 58
2. 33 − 12 = 21
3. 24 + 33 + 12 = 69
4. 12 − 9 = 3
5. 46 − 35 = 11
6. 35 + 50 = 85
7. 24 + 50 = 74
8. 74 − 12 = 62
9. Talia; 85 − 62 = 23 more

p. 64 — Missing Digits
A. 40 + 24 = 64   B. 87 − 72 = 15
C. 87 − 51 = 36   D. 49 − 27 = 22
E. 19 + 20 = 39   F. 42 + 14 = 56
G. 94 − 23 = 71   H. 81 − 50 = 31
I. 13 + 23 = 36   J. 45 + 14 = 59
K. 91 − 60 = 31   L. 55 + 23 = 78
M. 32 + 36 = 68
N. 136 + 502 = 638
O. 821 − 200 = 621
P. 588 − 152 = 436
Q. 362 + 637 = 999
R. 211 + 145 = 356

CD-4333 *Brain-Boosting Math*

p. 66 — Knock 'Em Down

A. 748 (color), 584 (color), 589, 476 (color)

B. 357 (color), 488, 268 (color), 859

C. 669, 569, 369, 579 (color all)

p. 67 — Penguins

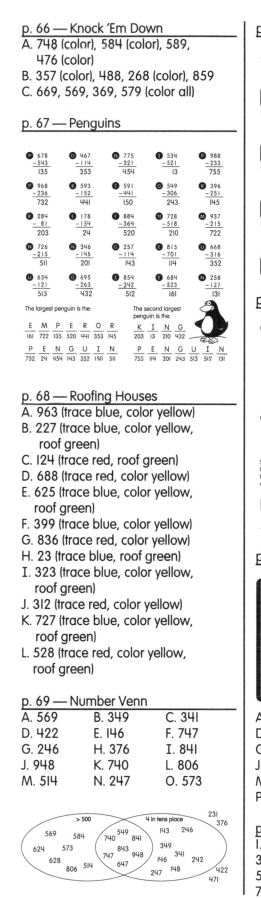

P 678 −543 135	**O** 467 −114 353	**N** 775 −321 454	**I** 534 −521 13	**P** 988 −233 755
P 968 −236 732	**E** 593 −152 441	**T** 591 −441 150	**G** 549 −306 243	**R** 396 −251 145
K 284 −81 203	**E** 178 −154 24	**E** 884 −364 520	**N** 728 −518 210	**M** 937 −215 722
N 726 −215 511	**N** 346 −145 201	**G** 257 −114 143	**P** 815 −701 114	**U** 668 −316 352
I 634 −121 513	**G** 695 −263 432	**I** 854 −342 512	**I** 684 −523 161	**N** 258 −127 131

The largest penguin is the:

E M P E R O R
161 722 135 520 441 353 145

P E N G U I N
732 24 454 143 352 150 511

The second largest penguin is the:

K I N G
203 13 210 432

P E N G U I N
755 114 201 243 513 512 131

p. 68 — Roofing Houses

A. 963 (trace blue, color yellow)

B. 227 (trace blue, color yellow, roof green)

C. 124 (trace red, roof green)

D. 688 (trace red, color yellow)

E. 625 (trace blue, color yellow, roof green)

F. 399 (trace blue, color yellow)

G. 836 (trace red, color yellow)

H. 23 (trace blue, roof green)

I. 323 (trace blue, color yellow, roof green)

J. 312 (trace red, color yellow)

K. 727 (trace blue, color yellow, roof green)

L. 528 (trace red, color yellow, roof green)

p. 69 — Number Venn

A. 569   B. 349   C. 341
D. 422   E. 146   F. 747
G. 246   H. 376   I. 841
J. 948   K. 740   L. 806
M. 514   N. 247   O. 573

p. 70 — Pull It Apart

A. 72 + 82 can be written as:
7 tens + 2 ones
+ 8 tens + 3 ones
15 tens + 4 ones
Regroup: 1 + 5 + 4 = 154
hundreds tens ones

B. 97 + 72 can be written as:
9 tens + 7 ones
+ 7 tens + 2 ones
16 tens + 9 ones
Regroup: 1 + 6 + 9 = 169
hundreds tens ones

C. 68 + 71 can be written as:
6 tens + 8 ones
+ 7 tens + 1 ones
13 tens + 9 ones
Regroup: 1 + 3 + 9 = 139
hundreds tens ones

D. 39 + 42 can be written as:
3 tens + 9 ones
+ 4 tens + 2 ones
7 tens + 11 ones
Regroup: 0 + 8 + 1 = 81
hundreds tens ones

E. 54 + 38 can be written as:
5 tens + 4 ones
+ 3 tens + 8 ones
8 tens + 12 ones
Regroup: 0 + 9 + 2 = 92
hundreds tens ones

F. 57 + 28 can be written as:
5 tens + 7 ones
+ 2 tens + 8 ones
7 tens + 15 ones
Regroup: 0 + 8 + 5 = 85
hundreds tens ones

G. 61 + 29 can be written as:
6 tens + 1 ones
+ 2 tens + 9 ones
8 tens + 10 ones
Regroup: 0 + 9 + 0 = 90
hundreds tens ones

H. 73 + 18 can be written as:
7 tens + 3 ones
+ 1 tens + 8 ones
8 tens + 11 ones
Regroup: 0 + 9 + 1 = 91
hundreds tens ones

p. 71 — Old Bug

E 12 +29 41 blue	**S** 53 +74 127 blue	**A** 53 +65 118 blue	**H** 96 +90 186 red	**I** 83 +64 147 blue	**C** 72 +90 162 red
	O 28 +2 30 red	**P** 95 +72 167 blue	**G** 82 +99 181 blue	**K** 26 +68 94 red	**S** 59 +88 147 blue
P 38 +89 127 blue	**C** 48 +18 66 red	**O** 75 +39 114 red	**R** 93 +17 110 red	**I** 66 +49 115 blue	**C** 15 +7 22 red

Scientists found a fossil of a bug that is older than the dinosaurs. It was found in Ohio. Write the even answers on the lines below in order from smallest to largest. Write the correct letter above each number to find out what ancient bug is still with us today.

C O C K R O A C H
22 30 66 94 110 114 118 162 186

p. 72 — Picture It

1	2	3	4	5	6	7	8	9	10
11	12	13	14	15	16	17	18	19	20
21	22	23	24	25	26	27	28	29	30
31	32	33	34	35	36	37	38	39	40
41	42	43	44	45	46	47	48	49	50
51	52	53	54	55	56	57	58	59	60
61	62	63	64	65	66	67	68	69	70
71	72	73	74	75	76	77	78	79	80
81	82	83	84	85	86	87	88	89	90
91	92	93	94	95	96	97	98	99	100

A. 85   B. 73   C. 55
D. 23   E. 36   F. 87
G. 78   H. 69   I. 33
J. 86   K. 46   L. 56
M. 28   N. 38   O. 62
P. 84

p. 73 — Information

1. 12 − 8 = 4
2. 2 + 8 = 10
3. 5 − 3 = 2
4. 10 − 5 = 5
5. 8 + 10 = 18
6. 6 − 4 = 2
7. equal
8. 8 + 8 = 16

p. 74 — Pictograph

Draw 1 ☺ for every 2 students.

Activity	Number of Students
read	☺☺☺☺☺☺☺☺
finish work	☺☺
dice math	☺☺☺☺☺☺☺☺☺
color	☺☺☺
clean desk	☺☺☺
science project	☺☺☺☺☺☺

☺ = 2 students

1. If 10 students made an art project, how many faces would you make? __5__

2. If each ☺ = 2 students, how would you show 1 student? ___ (___ 9 students? ☺☺☺☺ (

3. Circle T for true or F for false.
   T (F) More students chose dice math than coloring.
   (T) F An equal number of students read as did the science project.
   (T) F Fewer students colored than cleaned desks.
   T (F) Ten more students finished work than read.

Draw 1 ☺ for every 3 students.

Activity	Number of Students
read	☺☺☺☺☺
finish work	☺☺
dice math	☺☺☺☺☺
color	☺☺☺☺
clean desk	☺☺
science project	☺☺☺☺☺

☺ = 3 students

p. 75 — Cookie Count

1. Phil; 16 cookies
2. Day One; 4 more
3. Jill and Will; 24 each or 48 total
4. 40 cookies
5.
6.

p. 76 — How Old Are You?

1. Use the raw data to fill in the tally chart.

Age	Number of Students
6	卌
7	卌 卌
8	川

2. Draw an X on the frequency table that matches your tally chart.

Age	Number of Students
6	5
7	10
8	3

3. Graphs will vary.
4. T, F, T, T, T, F

p. 77 — Simple Machines

Complete the graph using the information from the tally chart. Color 1 box for each machine Ryan saw. Use a different color for each type of machine.

Check each true statement.
✓ The wheel and axle was found most often.
___ Ryan found the lever the fewest number of times.
___ Screws were found more often than inclined planes.
✓ Pulleys and wedges were found an equal number of times.

CD-4333 *Brain-Boosting Math*

p. 78 — Lots of Fractions

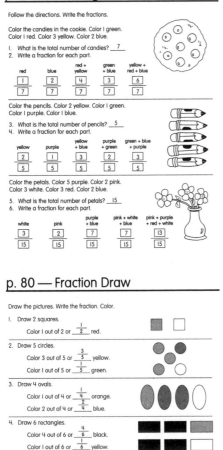

1. Total number of equal parts: __5__
   a. white = __2__ out of __5__
   b. dotted = __1__ out of __5__
   c. shaded = __2__ out of __5__
   d. white + dotted = __3__ out of __5__

	a	b	c	d
	$\frac{?}{5}$	$\frac{1}{5}$	$\frac{2}{5}$	$\frac{3}{5}$

2. Total number of equal parts: __3__
   a. dotted = __1__ out of __3__
   b. striped = __1__ out of __3__
   c. stars = __1__ out of __3__
   d. stars + striped = __2__ out of __3__

	a	b	c	d
	$\frac{1}{3}$	$\frac{1}{3}$	$\frac{1}{3}$	$\frac{2}{3}$

3. Total number of equal parts: __4__
   a. hearts = __2__ out of __4__
   b. striped = __1__ out of __4__
   c. white = __1__ out of __4__
   d. hearts + white = __3__ out of __4__

	a	b	c	d
	$\frac{2}{4}$	$\frac{1}{4}$	$\frac{1}{4}$	$\frac{3}{4}$

4. Total number of equal parts: __8__
   a. hearts = __3__ out of __8__
   b. stars = __1__ out of __8__
   c. shaded = __1__ out of __8__
   d. striped = __1__ out of __8__
   e. white = __2__ out of __8__
   f. striped + hearts = __4__ out of __8__
   g. white + hearts + stars = __6__ out of __8__

	a	b	c	d
	$\frac{3}{8}$	$\frac{1}{8}$	$\frac{1}{8}$	$\frac{1}{8}$

	e	f	g
	$\frac{2}{8}$	$\frac{4}{8}$	$\frac{6}{8}$

p. 79 — Coloring Fractions

Follow the directions. Write the fractions.

Color the candies in the cookie. Color 1 green.
Color 1 red. Color 3 yellow. Color 2 blue.

1. What is the total number of candies? __7__
2. Write a fraction for each part.

red	blue	red + yellow	green + blue	yellow + red + blue
$\frac{1}{7}$	$\frac{2}{7}$	$\frac{4}{7}$	$\frac{3}{7}$	$\frac{6}{7}$

Color the pencils. Color 2 yellow. Color 1 green.
Color 1 purple. Color 1 blue.

3. What is the total number of pencils? __5__
4. Write a fraction for each part.

yellow	purple	yellow + blue	purple + green	green + blue + purple
$\frac{2}{5}$	$\frac{1}{5}$	$\frac{3}{5}$	$\frac{2}{5}$	$\frac{3}{5}$

Color the petals. Color 5 purple. Color 2 pink.
Color 3 white. Color 3 red. Color 2 blue.

5. What is the total number of petals? __15__
6. Write a fraction for each part.

white	pink	purple + blue	pink + white + blue	pink + purple + red + white
$\frac{3}{15}$	$\frac{2}{15}$	$\frac{7}{15}$	$\frac{7}{15}$	$\frac{13}{15}$

p. 80 — Fraction Draw

Draw the pictures. Write the fraction. Color.

1. Draw 2 squares.
   Color 1 out of 2 or $\frac{1}{2}$ red.

2. Draw 5 circles.
   Color 3 out of 5 or $\frac{3}{5}$ yellow.
   Color 1 out of 5 or $\frac{1}{5}$ green.

3. Draw 4 ovals.
   Color 1 out of 4 or $\frac{1}{4}$ orange.
   Color 2 out of 4 or $\frac{2}{4}$ blue.

4. Draw 6 rectangles.
   Color 4 out of 6 or $\frac{4}{6}$ black.
   Color 1 out of 6 or $\frac{1}{6}$ yellow.

5. Draw 3 ovals.
   Color 1 out of 3 or $\frac{1}{3}$ green.
   Color 2 out of 3 or $\frac{2}{3}$ purple.

6. Draw 9 circles.
   Color 3 out of 9 or $\frac{3}{9}$ yellow.
   Color 4 out of 9 or $\frac{4}{9}$ orange.
   Color 1 out of 9 or $\frac{1}{9}$ green.

p. 81 — Fraction Twins

Drawings will vary but should be similar to those shown here.

A. $\frac{3}{4}$ have smiles
B. $\frac{1}{3}$ is white
C. $\frac{3}{6}$ are red
D. $\frac{1}{2}$ has hearts
E. $\frac{2}{3}$ have stars
F. $\frac{4}{5}$ are striped
G. $\frac{1}{4}$ is purple, $\frac{1}{4}$ is orange
H. $\frac{3}{7}$ are dotted, $\frac{1}{7}$ is green

pp. 82–83 — The Biggest Piece

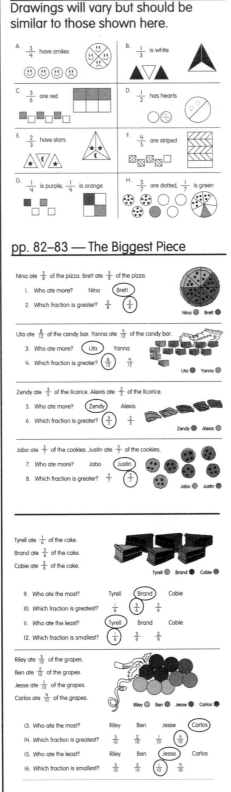

Nina ate $\frac{3}{8}$ of the pizza. Brett ate $\frac{5}{8}$ of the pizza.
1. Who ate more? Nina (Brett)
2. Which fraction is greater? $\frac{3}{8}$ ($\frac{5}{8}$)

Uta ate $\frac{8}{12}$ of the candy bar. Yanna ate $\frac{4}{12}$ of the candy bar.
3. Who ate more? (Uta) Yanna
4. Which fraction is greater? ($\frac{8}{12}$) $\frac{4}{12}$

Zendy ate $\frac{3}{5}$ of the licorice. Alexis ate $\frac{2}{5}$ of the licorice.
5. Who ate more? (Zendy) Alexis
6. Which fraction is greater? ($\frac{3}{5}$) $\frac{2}{5}$

Jabo ate $\frac{2}{7}$ of the cookies. Justin ate $\frac{5}{7}$ of the cookies.
7. Who ate more? Jabo (Justin)
8. Which fraction is greater? $\frac{2}{7}$ ($\frac{5}{7}$)

Tyrell ate $\frac{1}{6}$ of the cake.
Brand ate $\frac{3}{6}$ of the cake.
Cobie ate $\frac{2}{6}$ of the cake.
9. Who ate the most? Tyrell (Brand) Cobie
10. Which fraction is greatest? $\frac{1}{6}$ ($\frac{3}{6}$) $\frac{2}{6}$
11. Who ate the least? (Tyrell) Brand Cobie
12. Which fraction is smallest? ($\frac{1}{6}$) $\frac{3}{6}$ $\frac{2}{6}$

Riley ate $\frac{3}{10}$ of the grapes.
Ben ate $\frac{2}{10}$ of the grapes.
Jesse ate $\frac{1}{10}$ of the grapes.
Carlos ate $\frac{4}{10}$ of the grapes.
13. Who ate the most? Riley Ben Jesse (Carlos)
14. Which fraction is greatest? $\frac{3}{10}$ $\frac{2}{10}$ $\frac{1}{10}$ ($\frac{4}{10}$)
15. Who ate the least? Riley Ben (Jesse) Carlos
16. Which fraction is smallest? $\frac{3}{10}$ $\frac{2}{10}$ ($\frac{1}{10}$) $\frac{4}{10}$

p. 84 — Pop In

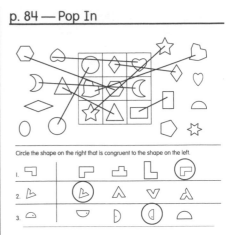

Circle the shape on the right that is congruent to the shape on the left.

1.
2.
3.

p. 85 — Sea Life

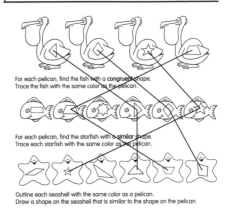

For each pelican, find the fish with a congruent shape.
Trace the fish with the same color as the pelican.

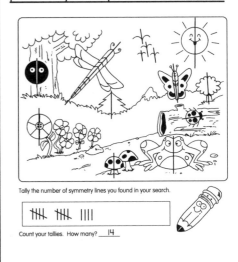

For each pelican, find the starfish with a similar shape.
Trace each starfish with the same color as the pelican.

Outline each seashell with the same color as a pelican.
Draw a shape on the seashell that is similar to the shape on the pelican.

p. 86 — Symmetry Search

Tally the number of symmetry lines you found in your search.

|||| |||| ||||

Count your tallies. How many? __14__

CD-4333 *Brain-Boosting Math*

p. 87 — Drawing Symmetry

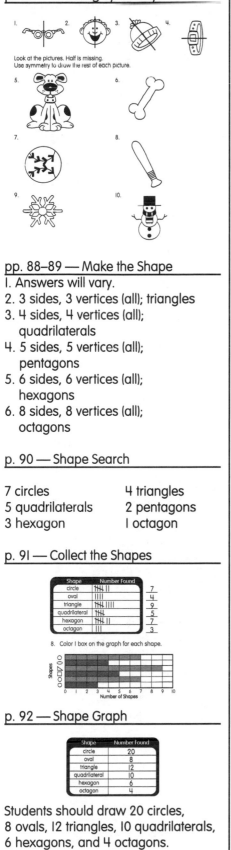

Look at the pictures. Half is missing.
Use symmetry to draw the rest of each picture.

pp. 88–89 — Make the Shape

1. Answers will vary.
2. 3 sides, 3 vertices (all); triangles
3. 4 sides, 4 vertices (all);
   quadrilaterals
4. 5 sides, 5 vertices (all);
   pentagons
5. 6 sides, 6 vertices (all);
   hexagons
6. 8 sides, 8 vertices (all);
   octagons

p. 90 — Shape Search

7 circles	4 triangles
5 quadrilaterals	2 pentagons
3 hexagon	1 octagon

p. 91 — Collect the Shapes

Shape	Number Found	
circle	𝍸𝍸 II	7
oval	IIII	4
triangle	𝍸𝍸 IIII	9
quadrilateral	𝍸𝍸	5
hexagon	𝍸𝍸 II	7
octagon	III	3

8. Color 1 box on the graph for each shape.

p. 92 — Shape Graph

Shape	Number Found
circle	20
oval	8
triangle	12
quadrilateral	10
hexagon	6
octagon	4

Students should draw 20 circles,
8 ovals, 12 triangles, 10 quadrilaterals,
6 hexagons, and 4 octagons.

p. 93 — 3-D Shapes Venn Diagram

pp. 94–95 — 3-D Shapes

1. 6; 12; 8	2. 5; 8; 5
3. 5; 9; 6	4. 1; 0; 0
5. 2; 0; 0	6. 0; 0; 0
7. 1; 0; 0	8. 6; 12; 8
9.	

Shape	Number of Corners	Number of Edges	Number of Faces
cone	0	0	1
cube	8	12	6
cylinder	0	0	2
hemisphere	0	0	1
rectangular prism	8	12	6
sphere	0	0	0
square pyramid	5	8	5
triangular prism	6	9	5

10. 3; cone, cylinder, hemisphere
11. 2; square pyramid, triangular prism
12. 4; cube, rectangular prism, square
    pyramid, triangular prism

p. 96 — Picnic Blankets
Answers will vary.

p. 97 — Mouse House

1. 72 tiles	2. 72¢
3. 18 tiles	4. 90¢
5. 8 tiles	6. 80¢
7. Answers will vary.	

p. 99 — Capacity Creature

A. 2	B. 2	C. 4	D. 4
E. 8	F. 16	G. 8	H. 2

I. No. A quart is only 4 cups.
   Need 5 cups.
J. No. A gallon is only 16 cups.
   Need 22 cups.

p. 100 — Inching Along

A. 2 in.	B. 6 in.
C. 1 in.	D. 7 in.
E. 3 in.	F. Answers will vary.
G. inches	H. miles
I. feet	J. inches
K. miles	L. inches

p. 101 — Centimeter Search

A. 15 cm	B. 9 cm
C. 4 cm	D. 11 cm
E. 2 cm	F. 6 cm
G. 17 cm	

H, I. Answers will vary.

p. 102 — Pan Balance

1. less than 17 grams
2. equal to 23 grams
3. more than 55 grams
4. less than 46 grams
5. equal to 10 grams

p. 103 — Money Match

p. 104 — Money Draw

1. 16¢	2. 20¢	3. 25¢
4. 45¢	5. 17¢	6. 40¢

p. 105 — Who Has More?

Count each group of coins. Write the value.

D 26 ¢	E 18 ¢	M 41 ¢
S 75 ¢	E 60 ¢	I 65 ¢
T 8 ¢	H 11 ¢	I 27 ¢

What is the smallest U.S. coin?
Write the coin values from smallest to largest on the lines below.
Write the letter that goes with each amount in the box.

8	11	18	26	27	41	60	65	75
T	H	E	D	I	M	E	I	S

Explain the answer. _____
The penny is the smallest in value but the dime is the smallest in size.

p. 106 — Money Comparisons

1. 40¢ > 25¢
2. 50¢ = 50¢
3. 20¢ < 25¢
4. 30¢ > 25¢
5. 80¢ > 75¢
6–8. Answers will vary.

p. 107 — Which Coins?

Answers will vary. Other combinations are possible.

1. 3 nickels OR 1 dime, 1 nickel OR 1 dime, 5 pennies
2. 2 nickels OR 10 pennies OR 1 nickel, 5 pennies
3. 8 nickels OR 1 quarter, 3 nickels
4. 1 dime OR 2 nickels OR 1 nickel, 5 pennies OR 10 pennies
5. 1 quarter, 4 nickels OR 9 nickels
6. 1 quarter, 6 dimes OR 3 quarters, 1 dime
7. 2 dimes, 3 pennies OR 23 pennies
8. 2 nickels, 3 pennies OR 13 pennies
9. 10 nickels, 3 pennies OR 2 quarters, 3 pennies

p. 108 — Coin Count

1. 5 pennies; 5¢
2. 8 dimes; 80¢
3. 11 nickels; 55¢
4. 9 pennies; 9¢
5. 3 nickels; 15¢
6. 4 dimes; 40¢

p. 109 — Money Graph

1. Make a tally chart.

Coin	Number of Coins
quarter	III
dime	THL IIII
nickel	THL IIII
penny	THL THL THL

2. Make a frequency table.

Coin	Number of Coins
quarter	3
dime	9
nickel	9
penny	15

3. 3; 75¢
4. 9; 90¢
5. 9; 45¢
6. 15; 15¢
7. pennies
8. dimes
9. dimes and nickels
10. 6

p. 110 — Money Matrix

	25¢	30¢	15¢
Art	✓	X	X
Mat	X	✓	X
Sal	X	X	✓

1. Mat
2. Sal
3. Art

	21¢	27¢	18¢
Bit	X	X	✓
Rif	X	✓	X
Sip	✓	X	X

4. Bit
5. Rif
6. Sip

p. 111 — River Race

A. 1, 2, 3, 4, 5, 6, 7, 8, 9, 10
B. 2, 4, 6, 8, 10, 12, 14, 16, 18, 20
C. 3, 6, 9, 12, 15, 18, 21, 24, 27, 30
D. 4, 8, 12, 16, 20, 24, 28, 32, 36, 40
E. 5, 10, 15, 20, 25, 30, 35, 40, 45, 50

p. 112 — They Each Have . . .

1. 9 + 9 = 18 apples
   2 x 9 = 18 apples
2. 3 + 3 + 3 + 3 + 3 + 3 = 18 letters
   6 x 3 = 18 letters
3. 2 + 2 + 2 = 6 stripes
   3 x 2 = 6 stripes
4. 1 + 1 + 1 + 1 + 1 + 1 + 1 = 7 stamps
   7 x 1 = 7 stamps

p. 113 — What If There's More?

1. 8, 10, 12, 14, 16, 18
2. 9, 12, 15, 18, 21, 24, 27
3. 12, 16, 20, 24, 28, 32, 36
4. 5, 10, 15, 20, 25, 30, 35, 40, 45
Multiplication problems will vary.

p. 114 — Angles and Sides

A. 8 sides, 8 angles
B. 20 sides, 20 angles
C. 0 sides, 0 angles
D. 6 sides, 6 angles
E. 21 sides, 21 angles
F. 0 sides, 0 angles
G. 24 sides, 24 angles
H. 15 sides, 15 angles
I. 24 sides, 24 angles
J. 18 sides, 18 angles

p. 115 — Draw the Sets

Drawings will vary but should match descriptions.

1. 8; 4 x 2 = 8
2. 6; 6 x 1 = 6
3. 16; 2 x 8 = 16
4. 18; 9 x 2 = 18
5. 9; 1 x 9 = 9
6. 40; 8 x 5 = 40
7. 21; 7 x 3 = 21
8. 20; 5 x 4 = 20
9. 14; 2 x 7 = 14
10. 24; 6 x 4 = 24
11. 12; 4 x 3 = 12
12. 18; 3 x 6 = 18

p. 116 — Filling Sets

Row 2: 8; 2 x 4 = 8
Row 3: 12; 6 x 2 = 12
Row 4: 12; 4 x 3 = 12
Row 5: 5; 5 x 1 = 5
Rows 6–10: Answers will vary.
1–4. Drawings will vary.

p. 117 — Let's Share

1. 2; no
2. 2; yes, 1
3. 1; no
4. 5; no
5. 2; yes, 1
6. 3; no
7. 3; yes, 1
8. 2; yes, 1

p. 118 — Fishbowl

Each fishbowl should contain the following:

1. 4 snails
2. 2 yellow fish
3. 6 marbles
4. 9 green fish
5. 2 plants
6. 3 rocks
7. 1 starfish
8. 5 red fish

p. 119 — Picnic at the Beach

1. 2 shovels each
2. 3 windows each
3. 5 ants each
4. 4 seeds each
5. Answers will vary.
Picture should include objects in sets as described.

p. 120 — Organization

Answers will vary.

1. 2 bags of 12; 3 bags of 8; 4 bags of 6; 6 bags of 4; 8 bags of 3; 12 bags of 2
2. 2 boxes of 10; 4 boxes of 5; 5 boxes of 4; 10 boxes of 2
3. 2 shelves of 6; 3 shelves of 4; 4 shelves of 3; 6 shelves of 2
4. 2 cups of 14; 4 cups of 7; 7 cups of 4; 14 cups of 2
5. 2 plates of 8; 4 plates of 4; 8 plates of 2
6. 2 groups of 9; 3 groups of 6; 6 groups of 3; 9 groups of 2

CD-4333 *Brain-Boosting Math*